ALICE TAYLOR

I was born on a hillside farm in North Cork near the Kerry border overlooking an inspirational view from the McGillycuddy Reeks to the Galtee Mountains; it was akin to looking out at a giant watercolour painting. This farm and amazing landscape were the inspiration for my first six books and maybe, in many ways, for all my books. When I married a wonderful man I came to live in the little village of Innishannon in West Cork, and have been here ever since. Innishannon continued the inspiration begun on the home farm. It was a busy life, running the village shop, post office and a guest house, and rearing children, as well as being involved in all village activity. I love this village and have written about it in *The Village* and *The Parish*. For many years I was part of a busy, crowded household. I love gardening, painting and writing, and have two lively black dobermann dogs who keep me company.

The Gift
of a Garden

Alice Taylor
Photographs by Emma Byrne

BRANDON

First published 2013 by
Brandon
an imprint of The O'Brien Press Ltd.
12 Terenure Road East, Rathgar,
Dublin 6, Ireland.

Tel: +353 1 4923333; Fax: +353 1 4922777
E-mail: books@obrien.ie.
Website: www.obrien.ie
Reprinted 2013.

ISBN: 978-1-84717-581-6

2 3 4 5 6 7 8
13 14 15 16 17 18

Printed and bound in Poland by Białostockie Zakłady Graficzne S.A.
The paper used in this book is produced
using pulp from managed forests

The O'Brien Press receives assistance from

DEDICATION

FOR JACKY – THANK YOU FOR THE GIFT OF YOUR GARDEN
AND TO ELLIE, WHO SHINES SUNBEAMS AMONGST THE FLOWERS

CONTENTS

INTRODUCTION

All my ills
My garden spade can heal

Welcome to my garden. Just inside the gate, hand-painted on a rickety piece of timber, is a little sign: Miracles only grow where you plant them. I saw it in a garden centre and could not resist it. This garden is full of my lack of resistance. I have no in-depth gardening knowledge and I work on impulse. Gardening friends bequeath, and I glean stray bits of knowledge from irresistible glossy gardening magazines and unbelievable TV gardening make-over programmes.

So my gardening expertise, acquired through trial and error, is nurtured by the wonderful pleasure that I have discovered in simply digging the earth. Where does that satisfaction come from? Maybe it is the farmer in me, having grown up on a farm. But we have all sprung from the land, descended from the stock of potato-picking ancestors. Maybe buried deep in each of us is the secret need to cultivate the soil. Digging the earth breathes life back into us.

Your garden reflects your personality. Mine is a picture of organised chaos. No law and order here! As I am by nature a tidy, well-organised individual, maybe my garden tells me that the inner me is an exuberant, untidy soul trying to break out. It is to this haven that I come when the other world gets too much for me, when my energy levels are down. I stumble in the gate and the garden silently reaches out its arms and says: Welcome back to your true home, my friend.

After the first warm embrace, it leads me along its winding paths where old companions nod in welcome. Ours is a friendship of scent and sight, and I know and understand every angle and hue of my dear plant friends. We have lived together for years. They absorb my agitation and as I meander around among them they untie my knots. This is where my mental reflexology happens. The plants that are in full flower dance with delight and ignite a flame of joy in me. For others the show is over and they are happy to take a back seat. Plants know that there is a time for each one of them

to be the star performer and a time to stand back; they are gracious beings. These are my close companions.

I am not the first gardener here. I inherited this garden from Uncle Jacky, who gardened here until he died in his late seventies over thirty years ago. This was his patch of the world and he gardened it with loving kindness. How do I know this? Because this little garden exudes the love he planted here. He created a healing place, a comforter – his '*flaitheaseen*' as he called it, his 'little bit of heaven'. This was his, and is now my '*flaitheaseen*'. How do you thank somebody for such a legacy? For such a gift? Maybe I can thank Uncle Jacky by passing the happiness of his little heaven on to you? Maybe I can plant the spirit of his garden into this little book, and then Uncle Jacky's legacy will never be lost and will bring joy forever.

Now, though a garden is definitely a thing of beauty and a joy forever, it is also a thing of beauty and a *job* forever! But that is part of its magic. A garden is a living, constant friend who waits lovingly for you, and when you come back it reaches out, claiming your mind and body to the exclusion of all else, but claiming your attention and your labours too. It is both a mind-cleanser and a back-breaker! Sometimes, when you're bending over the ground for too long, you think that a back with two iron hinges would be a blessing.

I am not a knowledgeable gardener, but this is not a book about gardening, rather a book about the comfort and sustenance that can be got from gardening and from the earth, about the wonderful pleasures and fulfilment that I get from my garden, that I hope to share with you. The earth is a sustainer. It engenders and sows within us a deep sense of endurance and working with it cultivates our basic instincts of self-worth and tolerance.

This garden has given me so much joy, and now I will try to give thanks by transplanting that gift into words.

Maybe I should have begun this book in January at the beginning of the year, but it is now August and the idea has just blossomed. But then, January is a bleak, barren month and August is full of bounty and exuberance. Surely a better time to begin? The well organised, tidy me would have begun at the beginning of the year, but it is my gardening soul that is going to write this book and so we take a leap of faith into the middle rather than the beginning.

I have no idea where the book will take us. The garden itself, and my joy in it and my work with it, will dictate the pace and direction. The book may fall into months or maybe seasons, who knows, but whatever way it will evolve I hope that Uncle Jacky's – and my – garden will glow between the pages and that you will find in it a comforting place to come to when the world is too much for you.

CHAPTER I

THE AWAKENING

The joy of anticipation
Awaiting dream realisation –
Looking forward is the fun
Of happy things yet to come.

The sun is pouring in the windows, filling the bedroom with golden light. Bedroom windows should,
if possible, face east because it is so good to wake up with the
warm sun on your face. It would be an added bonus if your
bedroom looked out over your garden, but as I am not so
blessed I roll out of bed and go out into the corridor where a
glass door opens on to a flat roof that overlooks the backyard
and garden.

The sight of the garden trees stretching to the skyline opens the windows into my soul. The flowers on the *Magnolia grandiflora* rest like large goose eggs nesting on glossy green leaves. The top branches of the golden frisia are glowing butter-yellow amid her more sober companions. A real show-off, with the fancy name *Robina pseudoacacia frisia*, you could forgive her anything because she is so happy. She makes you happy too. She brightens up the morning. I look down on the plants in the yard below too where the sweet peas climbing up the wall beside me give out their lovely scent. They fan my anticipation of the day.

Downstairs I put my breakfast on a tray to carry it out into the backyard. I believe in a good breakfast. It is more than a meal; it is a setter-upper for the day. So I dress my tray with a fancy tea towel strewn with wild flowers, a china cup and saucer, and a silver teapot. Fresh grapefruit, bowl of muesli, brown bread and homemade marmalade. Breakfast is ready. The backyard is glowing with flowers. I sit and soak in the vibrancy and the aromas that surround me. Flowers make you feel renewed and bring a smile to your face.

As I enjoy my breakfast I try not to look over to where I know the rose has been holding back. Some plants, like some people, come into flower late in their season. Their slow blossoming is tantalising, full of delayed promise. All during the previous week I kept a cautionary eye on her from a distance. I felt like a horse breeder waiting for a prize

mare to deliver a foal — though I do not even know her name and horse breeders can trace ancestry back to Adam or his horse equivalent.

I am a messy, *trí na chéile* gardener, with no track of my charges. They run wild and do what they like, and most of them are nameless. So my lady-in-waiting did not even have the dignity of a name and owed me nothing only the good bed of compost beneath her. She had actually been in the shadows, behind a huge lily that had over-wintered in the back porch and was then put out when the frosts were over. This lily had grown and grown, taking up a lot of space, and then produced nothing. She was like some people we all know. So when I had discovered that the lily was much ado about nothing, I chopped off her head! Maybe Henry VIII should have been a gardener; what a lot of wives that would have saved.

To fill the vacant space left by the beheaded lily, my nameless rose moved forward into centre court. She stood demurely shrouded in dark, glistening leaves, doing very little but promising much. It would have seemed intrusive to have gone across the yard and to have stood vulgarly awaiting her unveiling. But from her rich green foliage, you somehow felt that she was going to put on a dazzling display.

Yesterday it rained non-stop. It should not rain like this in August and I was not sure if the earth was soaking it up like a thirsty drunk or outraged at this ravaging of its overgrown finery. The petunias certainly collapsed in misery, their delicate petticoats dripping forlornly over the edge of their urn. But the leaves of the trees glistened in appreciation and the hydrangeas straightened their bending backs as the moisture went straight down their wilting spines.

I forgot, last evening, to check on my nameless rose. That happens in the garden – in my garden anyway. You get so taken up with one *protégé* that you somehow forget the others. Then the forgotten ones catch you unawares and you gasp in delight – something beautiful took place while your attention was somewhere else.

Now I glance across the yard. The miracle has happened! Breakfast is forgotten. She has blossomed. The unveiling had taken place overnight or in the early dawn. I walk towards her in reverence. She is simply stunning in her perfection. Not pink, red or orange, but a combination of the best of all three colours. Saucer-large and luscious, she rests on her rich, satin foliage like a jewel on a dark pillow. She is breathtaking. I stand in awe and soak up the moment. Moments like this are why people garden – dig until their backs break and prune until their arms ache. And then the garden decides it's payback time and puts on a shameless display of enticement. It lights up some part of your inner being and you know that

life does not get any better than this. You are looking at a masterpiece, though unlike a Monet this is not permanent. It is a beautiful transient ballet, and for a brief moment you are the dancer and the rose lifts you into a spiral of enchantment. I gently move closer to my beautiful nameless rose and her fragrance – light and delicate – wafts up my nose. How can a rose look so beautiful *and* smell so good? Even in the rose world life does not dole out its favours equally. I stand back in appreciation. Beauty such as this has to be savoured and reverenced. It is indeed a moment for taking the time to smell the roses.

Then I feel the need to share this magic moment. But no one is available to me except a son who is into football and veteran cars. I haul him across the yard. He gazes wordlessly and his silence speaks volumes.

'Wow!' he breathes finally.

As a young lad he had gardened with Uncle Jacky. When we depart this earth we can pass on many inheritances, but maybe an appreciation of the world's beauty is one of the most valuable treasures we can leave behind. Thank you, Uncle Jacky.

CHAPTER 2

A JUG OF FLOWERS

Give me a bunch
Of dew-fresh flowers
What if they will not last
I cannot live in the future
The present is all I ask.

One of the best things about gardening is the inducement to wander around aimlessly. Most mornings I meander, sometimes in my nightdress, out into the backyard and up into the garden just to see how they all are after the night. A morning walk around the garden is totally different to an evening walk; an evening walk is a winder-downer, but a morning walk is a waker-upper. In the morning they are all fresh and vibrant; they are standing tall and refreshed after the dampness of the night, and they tell you: Wake up and dance with us, it's the start of a new day. But you must be careful because a garden is like a demanding child always looking for attention, and before you know what you're doing you're dead-heading or propping up a plant that has lost its grip. But my garden and I are on very familiar terms, so now I tell them: Shut up! This is my time. I'll come to you later.

Then, on this lovely late summer morning, I go up the stone steps beside Jacky's apple tree and stop dead in my tracks: where is that heavenly smell coming from? I sniff around like a cocker spaniel. Then a flash of yellow catches my eye and I realise that a beautiful lily has come into full bloom and is pouring her essence over all her neighbours. She is standing demurely beside a statue of one of the Three Wise Men from a Christmas crib who has found his way into the garden. He was rescued from a skip, looking the worse for wear after years in a dusty loft over our church, and I restored his regal regalia. Too big for domestic confines, he had come out into the garden. It was a wise decision, because now here he was, basking in the aroma of this beautiful lily and sheltering under the arm of an over-reaching hydrangea. He was a long way from Bethlehem, but then the Lord is found in strange places!

I wander further, just to see how the rest of them up in the grove are looking after the night and to see if there have

been any more miracles. Then back down by another path. I like meandering paths around a garden; they lead you into hidden corners. The pure white stock are poking their heads out through their green jumpers and saying: Look at us, look at us, aren't we beautiful? And they are! I stand and admire them, and sniff their musky smell. These are the old reliables of late summer, coming every year with minimum fuss. There are two groups of them, at either side of the winding path up to my St Joseph statue; I notice that the ones to the left are stronger and putting on a better display than those to the right. It is one of the mysteries of gardening why this should be so. After all, they are within a few feet of each other. It's all about location, location, location. Could it be that the soil is more moist to the left and they like that? Anyway, that is the way it is with gardening. Sometimes it is beyond all understanding, which is why it never loses its magic.

Behind the white stock is the deep red stock and they are aglow with staunch rigour. 'Now, my dears,' I tell them, 'I will get the pruner and take you into the kitchen. You will brighten up my day.' I collect my pruner out of a bucket hanging on the gate and snip the long-legged red blossoms. There is a great feeling about gently snipping fresh garden flowers and bearing them into the kitchen for arranging.

The first decision to be made in the kitchen is the container. Every arrangement, no matter how humble, deserves a suitable receptacle to show it off to advantage. These flowers are long-stemmed and upright, so they need a deep container. My eyes flit along the dresser and rest on Aunty Peg's jug. Perfect! This jug is older than myself, and is tall, white and stately, with a gold cord around its middle. I remember my husband, Gabriel, telling me that as a child he was often sent across the road with it to old Mrs O'Halloran's dairy for milk and warned not to break that jug. Looking at the lovely old jug, I wonder how is it that in those far-off days, when they did not, as far as I know, study design, they got things so right. Good design, I always think, is just easy on the eye. And this jug has a simple elegance. Full of milk it speaks of plenty, and full of flowers it enhances the contents. I ease off the lower leaves and the flowers arrange themselves in the jug. Flowers and jug form a complete whole and fill the kitchen with the spirit of the garden. There is nothing more uplifting than a bunch of fresh garden flowers on your kitchen table. They comfort and massage your spirit in a simple, happy way.

CHAPTER 3

HEAVY DRINKERS!

The male of our species has been heard to describe some females as 'high maintenance'. Well, hanging baskets are the high-maintenance ladies of the gardening world. They need to be constantly fed and watered. As their tops, bottoms and sides are exposed to the drying effects of sun and air, they are perpetually in a state of thirst. Of course, no flower or plant should be expected to perform in mid-air. It's a crazy concept. How would we like to live like flying saucers? It doesn't make any sense. But we gardeners do not always behave sensibly – and some evenings when I stagger in from the garden with a lame leg, a bent back and a crooked neck, I question my own sanity. If my non-gardening neighbour happens to come in, I can see that she has questions about it as well. She is wondering how did this friend, who had been sane for years, suddenly turn into this lunatic gardener. I blame my mother. After all, that's what mothers are for – to soak up the guilt of their offspring who want to feel good about themselves. We have all heard the remark: what would you expect with a mother like hers?

It is definitely my mother's fault because even in the midst of her hard struggle for survival in the hungry thirties, forties and fifties of the last century, she still managed to garden around our ancient farmhouse in the wilds of North Cork. She bought packets of seeds and nurtured them in beds along the front of our house. She got slips from neighbours and as nobody knew their botanical name, these plants were called after the donor. So we had 'Jer Lucy's bush', which in later years I discovered to be an escalonia, and 'Mary O's shrub', which turned out to be a hydrangea, and 'the bell tree', which I later discovered was a fuchsia, and 'Grandmother Taylor's roses', which are still nameless but remembered fondly for their wonderful scent.

Gardening is all about smells and memories. Maybe the desire to garden comes from our roots – so if you want to give your children a gift for life and a place to retreat to when the world gets too much for them, get them planting. Not easy to convert them, and if you finish up with one child interested out of six, you have done well. Nowadays, with limited-edition families, your chances of success could be reduced – or maybe increased as smaller numbers may mean greater quality gardening time. But even without immediate success, the chances are that if you garden, they too will garden. Eventually. We all turn into our parents in the end!

Despite all my protestations about hanging baskets, this year I fell victim to that mania. I cornered a reluctant son to erect seven of them around my backyard. When I need a job done I am a great exploiter of filial guilt. Now with its seven swinging baskets, my backyard resembles my idea of the Hanging Gardens of Babylon. Unfortunately, this yard is best described as a haggard rather than a swanky patio area; it is not tiled or flagged, but covered in ancient concrete that has long given

up the struggle to impress. It is constantly under threat from grass that tries to make a comeback and weeds that feel it is rightly theirs. My excuse for not doing anything to improve it is that with so many pots and containers overflowing with all kinds of everything, there is very little of the actual yard to be seen anyway.

Some of the containers are enormous, like the two redundant black water tanks and Aunty Peg's old bath tub, several barrels and a miscellaneous collection of pots of varying sizes and different stages of antiquity. Then there are two retired wheelbarrows, one with vertigo and the other with advanced arthritis. My collection is like a long-tailed, colourful family. Some, due to a misspent youth and missing parts, are not the stuff of family pride, and need to be kept out of sight in shady corners. No way could I push any of them around simply to posh up the yard to impress the neighbours, as they would totally collapse.

To add to the confusion, there is also an upstairs-downstairs element to the backyard. The back porch has a flat roof and up on top of that is another garden. Sometimes in midsummer the two merge as the upstarts below reach up and high flyers above trail down, and then the hanging baskets link both, helping to promote a more just society.

Container gardening has its challenges, but also its rewards, as every container is a miniature garden in itself. Creating a container garden is like painting a picture, and each can tell a different story. Window boxes, however, tend to be a replica of each other, especially if you have a lot of them. I live on a village corner, so I have window boxes outside on the sills facing south and east, while those in the backyard face north. This leaves me with too many windows boxes, and over the years their journey has been one of many triumphs and disasters. Petunias are beautiful but petulant, and if ignored even for a very short period they turn into slimy sluts. Busy Lizzies are raging alcoholics and will not cooperate without a constant supply of liquids. Geraniums are good and I even got away with over-wintering them outside for many years, but then came minus ten degrees one year and they turned into a soggy mess.

So now I have begun a love affair with begonias. Watching them sprout from wizened little corms into huge, flowery floozies is delightful. They really come into profusion in July and August. If well fed and watered, they mature into big Rubens women with huge, luxuriant bosoms overhanging their boxes and sprouting giant leaves out of deep cleavages. They require no dead-heading, but exercise no self control either and simply drop their over-ripe blooms carelessly from their boxes onto the footpath below, turning the world around them into confetti-strewn aisles. If you forget to water them, they are very forgiving and will simply drink deeply when you do remember them, and recover. Their exuberance is unquenchable as they sprawl in unseemly fashion all over the place. I love them.

Sometimes, early in the morning, before I come down-stairs, I water the upstairs window boxes and then I go out on to the roof of the back porch to do the upstairs garden. Here the colourful begonias overflow their boxes and reach down to the lower orders beneath them. The upright canna, however, stand tall and arrogant in their big pots, but when they at last flower it is worth waiting for their dramatic appearance. The green ones are not as big a statement as their brown brothers, who strut on top of the roof like Nazi lookout guards, though instead of blazing bullets they shoot brilliant orange blooms. They are a force to be reckoned with, and I constantly salute their imperious presence. With them are two black men: these were bought on impulse at an antique auction where I went to bid for a garden seat. As I paid up after the auction I wondered why I had bid for them, and when I came home the wonder grew. They did not look right anywhere in the garden, so they finished up on the roof where their strange, flowing cloaks and arched wings intro-duced a multi-cultural heavenly dimension.

This year I put trellis on the wall up there on the rooftop garden. This area lies outside my bedroom window, so I set sweet peas there, hoping their lovely scent would invade the upstairs rooms. Because they stood in full sunshine, they got off to a great start, but then due to a temporary distraction I forgot to water them – and, oh boy, did they sulk. It took long weeks of coaxing with regular feeding and watering before they recovered their good humour and forgave me. But once back in action, they were worth all the effort. The magic of sweet peas, of course, is that the more you cut them the more they bloom, and every few days I would put a fresh bunch by my bed and on the kitchen table, and they generously filled the place with the most wonderful fragrance.

Late in the evening you turn into a night nurse for the plants, doing the rounds, watering and caring, and because watering is life-giving it can be very therapeutic to both giver and receiver – and these patients are very appreciative. They fill up your senses with their wonderful *pot pourri* of smells, especially the night-scented stock, whose name tells its story. Having taken care of my friends in the backyard, the garden is next in line.

Opening out of the backyard, but totally separate from it, is the garden. A hedge of miscellaneous shrubs and trees divides the two, and in between is the back entrance to the shop, where deliveries come and go. So my garden could be described as an enclosed, walled garden, though that description might be a bit fanciful. To the right of the gate is an old stone wall, which is a high-rise apartment block for uncountable numbers of slugs who, like a silent army, emerge at night to attack my hostas, dahlias and anything else that takes their fancy. They are ravenous monsters with insatiable appetites, and they and I wage non-stop warfare, which they usually win. As I water my garden in the dusk I know that they are rallying the troops to march out once I have retired for the night.

I go along dead-heading and checking for the overburdened or top-heavy who may need a little prop. This is the time for gentle guidance and support for the plants, and, for me, a winding down of the day. The garden at this hour is a magical place, full of shadows and mysteries, and sometimes a late-night bird is still chirping away. I walk carefully under the Golden King holly tree where I know the two doves have already retreated for the night. One night I forgot about them and pulled out the prop for the clothes line that leans against that tree – they crashed out, belting their wings against the branches, and if they could use bad language they would have screamed obscenities at me. Now I am careful not to disturb the sleeping pair.

Having gone all around the garden, I stand at the gate and the peace of this much-loved place seeps over me. The light from the street lamps filters in through the trees. I come down through the backyard, where in the semi-dark all the different containers are blended beautifully together in a fusion of smells and muted colours. It is time to say good night.

CHAPTER 4

THE SILENT PEOPLE

She was the first silent woman to come into the garden and she came in a roundabout fashion. She did not walk in, but was carried by the head and legs: DJ had her by the legs and I had her by the scruff of the neck. Before you begin to think that this was a mauling of the innocent, I hasten to add that she is made of stone.

We had held a Meet the Neighbours night in the parish hall and, along with plants and flowers, DJ from the local garden centre had brought her to decorate the hall. When the night was over and DJ was collecting his bits and pieces, the nude lady looked in mute appeal in my direction. It was understandable that she had fallen for Innishannon and simply did not want to go home, and so DJ and I struck a deal and she was borne into my garden. Pristine white, she did not settle in easily and screamed at me across the greenery, so much so, that I almost contemplated sending her home, but always finished up thinking that she deserved one more chance and might finally settle. Mine is an old-fashioned, shaded bower, and I was not sure that a bright, brazen hussy with a bare bosom, balancing on one leg while she washed the other, quite fitted in. There was a lot of waltzing around the garden with her, and as she was a solid lady lacking flexibility, it was not exactly an elegant glide. With a reluctant son, I dragged her back and forth until we found a shaded corner against the western ditch. There, the son decided – right or wrong – she was to remain. He would not contemplate another move. So I had to accept that this was to be her final resting place.

But time sorts out most things and over the years the leaves dripped down on her, creating a soft green cloak, and ivy grew up her leg, and so she slowly turned from a erotic lady into a green nymph. A garden can work wonders: an outrageous hussy can become a demure lady! Eventually, a redundant arch placed over her became smothered in ivy, so she then had a discreet corner in which to complete her toiletries.

She was the first silent resident, and due to the cultural difficulties encountered in her resettlement, I had learned about the need for caution in choosing my new neighbours. Not everybody would fit in and be happy in my little corner of the world. So, further nomads seeking refuge would need to be viewed with caution. Would they fit in? Would they like me? Would I like them? It could take time before these questions would be answered, so adopting silent people into my garden could be a risk. A bit like marriage, it took time to discover if it worked well and if all were compatible. Selectivity and caution were to be the name of the game. Impulsive adoption was out. I could finish up with a cuckoo in the nest!

However, when I saw Red-haired Mary I forgot all my good resolutions and threw discretion to the winds. It was love at first sight. But she was demanding a sizeable bounty, far more than I was prepared to pay for a fancy woman. However, my birthday was coming up, and heavy hints were dropped, and they paid off because on the morning of the birthday Red-haired Mary came in the gate. Boy, had she class! Pure terracotta and bearing a flowerpot in one hand and a basket in the other, she fitted in immediately. With her trailing locks and flowing gown, she was a natural for the garden, where she stood demurely beneath a tree, glancing shyly at anyone coming through the garden gate.

She had more serious things on her mind than the hussy across the garden. When her flowerpot and basket were filled with blooms, she could have been a lady of the manor, gathering flowers for the Great House. She was at ease, creating no sense of discord. However, in later years when greenery threatened to eclipse Mary, she had to be shifted. Easier said than done! There was more to my demure lady than met the eye. She dug her toes into the earth and refused to budge; it was a case of We Shall Not Be Moved. And when a hefty son decided otherwise, she left her toes behind her in the earth! But despite that, she still held her balance in her new position. She was a woman for all locations.

My two women were at opposite ends of the garden: DJ's woman was inside the western ditch and faced east, while Red-haired Mary was inside the high stone wall on the eastern side and faced west. Red-haired Mary did not even raise her head to look across at the naked lady. She treated her with the utmost disdain. They came from two different worlds.

But I felt that my garden might now benefit from a male presence. Sometimes, even in the plant world, a male and a female are needed to propagate the species – or at least to balance things out. But I did not want too robust a presence to disturb the tranquility of my quiet Eden, so I opted for a serene, saintly

presence. St Francis, I decided, would be my man. He loved birds of the feathered kind, and so was the ideal choice as the garden was the feeding and nesting place of so many birds. But where to find Francis was the question. Years previously I had gone to Assisi and brought home a little carved wooden one under my arm, but he was not for the great outdoors, and anyway that little Francis would be no match for the two women already in residence – especially DJ's woman, who might scare the living daylights out of him. So I was on the lookout for a big man.

My search took me to Glencomeragh, at the foot of Slieve na mBan in County Tipperary, where Fr Jimmy Brown runs a monastery and a farm. When I inquired about the prospects of sourcing a St Francis, I was asked: 'Would you settle for a Saint Joseph?' Strangely enough, I have always had a soft spot for Joseph. I felt that it could not have been easy for him to live with two of the biggest stars of Christendom. It was in the era before celebrity status became such a big deal, but still he must occasionally have felt over-shadowed in his family: not only was he married to the most perfect woman in Christendom, but his teenage son turned into a hippy and tried to convert the world. All parents know about the idealistic teenage son who wants to save the whale at the other end of the world while refusing to feed the dog behind the back door. So I had great sympathy for Joseph and was open to giving him a loving welcome. I went to view him behind the monastery. He was about the same height as myself and in his former home the nuns had painted him a pristine white, but on enquiry I discovered that he was carved out of Portland stone. So this Joseph was no lightweight and carrying him from mid-Tipperary to West Cork was going to be no mean feat. Fr Jimmy, as if reading my thoughts, informed me: 'Don't think for a minute, now, that you can throw him into the boot of a car and carry him home with you. You will need a trailer and a hoist.'

'How did you finish up with a spare Saint Joseph?' I inquired.

'His convent home closed down and he was homeless,' he told me.

I was happy to give St Joseph a home. It might not be orderly and well maintained like a convent, but as he was St Joseph the Worker I felt that he was coming to the right place. My garden is always full of jobs to be done and his presence might encourage industry.

Now, if you want to get a weighty job done, the first thing you need is a farmer – they have heavy machinery and they know how to use it. But he needs to be a smart, willing farmer. I am lucky enough to have one in the family. My niece married into a farm outside the village and her husband, Paddy, is an adopted son – so I acquainted Paddy with my problem, which he tackled with the methodology of a scientist.

'If you're bringing a solid stone man into your garden, he'll need a solid base. We'll have to dig a hole and give him a foundation.'

So, with the foundation laid, we headed for the Glen with a trailer and borrowed hoist. That is the blessing of the farming community – if one has it, they all have it. They still operate the barter system, so a hoist was acquired from a good neighbour who was into shifting old machinery.

Normally the car park of the Glen monastery would be chock-a-block with cars, but on this day Tipperary was playing a hurling match in Croke Park, so all of Tipp was in the capital, giving us the space to back right up to Joseph. By a process beyond my understanding, Joseph was hoisted into the trailer and we set out at a very slow pace back down to Innishannon. There he was lifted out of the trailer and on to the base of a combi, which is a rock-solid piece of wood edged with iron and mounted on wheels. Then, with more enlisted help, he was manoeuvred through the garden gate, up along the lawn and slowly edged on to the raised area in front of the Old Hall which borders our garden to the north and was once a Methodist preaching house. Then Joseph was carefully lowered on to his waiting platform. We all breathed a sigh of relief. Joseph had landed!

But, unfortunately, Joseph also came with a problem, the same problem as DJ's woman: he too was brilliant white and stood out like a sore thumb. But whereas DJ's woman was

man-made, Joseph was the real thing made of solid stone and all he needed to reveal his sterling qualities was to remove his overcoat, which he was tough enough to tolerate. And so began the long stripping down of Joseph. On the advice of an artist friend, I tackled him with a bucket of soapy water, a sponge and a small, blunt knife, and slowly the real Joseph emerged. Stripping him was a revelation. He was beautiful and became more so as his white coat slid to the ground around him. When I had finished, he looked great, and greater still as he mellowed with the years. His backdrop is the dark, ivy-clad wall of the Old Hall. This part of the garden had once been the site for our beehives, and as bees are regarded as sacred, at least Joseph was on holy ground, I felt, and maybe John Wesley comes out of the Old Hall at times and they discuss the state of religion in the world today?

Because he had worked with wood, I felt that Joseph should be surrounded by trees, so I dug up a gleditsia and an acer from the other side of the garden and enshrouded him with them. The gleditsia is a bright, lemon-coloured leafy tree that in summer drapes itself in clouds around Joseph, and with the acer forms a halo over his head. Several buddleias are planted near him too and in autumn butterflies flutter around him. A cloak of ivy has crept over his shoulder and a rambling rose is making its way up his long skirt. Joseph has grown into his surroundings.

Over the years other figures have arrived in the garden. A

sea-faring man with one leg stands inside the garden gate; it is a bit difficult to explain his presence, but he keeps a beady eye out for undesirables. Then, to counteract his wary presence, there is a beguiling little girl with a basket of flowers telling you that all is well in the garden. She was bought on impulse, as was a cloaked, saintly figure with long hair, bearing a book and quill, whom I found in an old farm shed in the Midlands. A visitor later introduced him to me as St John – I'd had no idea who he was and was glad to identify his benign presence. At a later date, two Wise Men joined him when they escaped from a skip and ran in the gate seeking refuge.

Sometimes it is questionable if I have a garden or a refugee centre for waifs and strays. But they all live happily together, and a brown deer that strayed in too sits on top of an old tree trunk and watches over the lot of them. I like to imagine that maybe at night, when my two dogs, Kate and Lolly, have gone to bed and the birds are asleep in their nests, all these people gather around the garden table and hold a silent conference.

CHAPTER 5

UNDER THE APPLE TREE

It was apple-picking day in the garden. The ancient apple tree, despite the fact that she is knotted with old age, had a huge crop. When I came to Innishannon in the early sixties, this tree, planted by Uncle Jacky as a young man, was fully grown, with its arms stretched out over the vegetable patches, and under it an old garden seat, where Jacky and Aunty Peg regularly sat to enjoy the delights of their garden. This was their favourite corner. In spring it sprouted daffodils around their seat and in summer it was smothered in roses. Dogs and hens slept and scratched around their feet. It was great then to sit here with them and chat. Looking back now, I realise that

I was young and restless and they were full of the wisdom of years of village shopkeeping and gardening. On warm, sunny days their visitors often sat here with them and talked for hours.

Every corner of their garden was in full production, providing a constant supply of food for the kitchen, and Aunty Peg's table was never without a vase of garden flowers. They used their garden to its utmost potential. The tree provided apples for baking, and for jams and jellies. Aunty Peg, of course, did not make ordinary apple tarts, she made her special apple cakes: they had lashings of butter, sugar and eggs, and layers of juicy apples. She baked them in big roasting tins, which she often forgot in the oven so they came out bubbling with over-cooked golden juices that flowed around the tin and sealed the edges of the cake with a crispy, amber coat.

Now I looked up fondly into the gnarled branches of this geriatric old friend. She and I had weathered many storms together. Uncle Jacky had rested beneath her sheltering branches in his last months when he had to have a leg amputated; the garden he had cared for over so many years comforted him then. When he died during a warm weekend in August, his garden nurtured Aunty Peg, who spent many hours sitting under this same apple tree. The silence of the garden was her haven then, and the seat under the old tree her healing place. The seat is still here, and on hot summer days it is still a restful, shaded corner in which to have tea in the garden.

But today was a work day. Over the past week I had watched the apples grow bigger and bigger, looking down at me reproachfully as if to say: Come on, get a move on, we need picking. They clung in clusters along her twisted branches, causing them to drape around her curving spine like a technicolour shawl. For weeks the blackbirds had turned the top branches into a highrise café where they enjoyed an early breakfast, and when a half-pecked apple thumped to the ground they had lunch and dinner at ground level. Crows quarrelled along the branches as they jockeyed for space to enjoy the juicy dessert. The little birds disappeared into her leaves and came out full-chested, with overloaded beaks. Bees and wasps buried themselves in the apples, with only their tails visible, and then flew low, laden with cargoes of apple juice.

I rounded up the nearest son to climb the tree with a bucket to collect the apples. At first that plan worked, but frustration at apples balancing on the tips of unreachable branches soon led to a shaking of this ancient lady until her fragile fingertips were forced to loosen their grip. Apples thumped down all around me and I knew that their storage days were shortened by such rough treatment. It called for fast kitchen action.

As we filled box after box with large, juicy apples, seg-regating them into bruised and non-bruised, it seemed almost unfair to rob all the high-rise diners of their bounty. But nature looks after her own and the topmost branches held on to big, unreachable prizes that would feed many high flyers in the weeks ahead.

The gathered apples nestled together in the boxes, some of them sheltering under still-attached leafy twigs. This old tree has filled many boxes in its lifetime. The planting of an apple tree is a great investment in the future; Uncle Jacky left a bountiful blessing for generations to come.

Stored apples have a wonderful smell, and the boxes stacked along a corridor behind the kitchen sent a waterfall of essences through the house. But they and I knew that time, especially for my bruised friends, is of the essence, so a big bake-up was on the horizon. But that's a job for a wet day when the world outside no longer beckons.

I am an avid listener to weather forecasts. Maybe it comes from having being reared on a farm where the weather dictated the work plan. Now it dictates my gardening plans and, in this case, my baking plans. So when I woke up one day to early-morning rain lashing against my window, the decision was made: baking day!

After breakfast I cleared the decks and brought the most damaged box of apples to the kitchen table. I am not a good apple peeler; I see it as simply a necessary evil for the baking of apple tarts. So I turned off my mind and got on with it. Maybe the radio might help, I thought, but after a few minutes listening to the financial troubles of the world I opted instead for a CD of Strauss music that my friend Annette had brought back to me when she attended a concert in Dublin – I just love people who bring you something they love themselves because if you are like-minded people the chances are that you receive a little gold mine. Strauss saw me through the peeling. I promised myself that when I was finished I would lie on the couch with a lavender pillow over my eyes and enjoy him in comfort.

But in the meantime, on with the job. First, two big Aunty Peg-style apple cakes in roasting tins, one for the Hospice coffee morning and the other for the Alzheimer's tea day that were coming up. Because I live in the centre of the village and have the space, I am the obvious choice to host these events, and we all enjoy the chat while we make money for the cause. The two biggies done, it was back to normal plates and I kept going in relays until the Aga said 'cool it', and refused to do any more. I lined up the remainder in the fridge until the Aga got her act together and warmed up again. By now the table and all the dresser ledges were full of golden tarts. By some miracle I had no burnt offering, simply because I kept my wits about me and had no stray callers.

But now both the Aga and myself were burnt out. After a quick tidy-up, I viewed my day's work in a kitchen saturated with the wonderful smell of baking. I felt virtuous and ful-filled. There is something about baking that satisfies the crea-tive juices and puts you at peace with the world. But my feet were complaining and my back aching. It was time for the lavender pillow and Johann Strauss.

CHAPTER 6

GARDENING WITH DOGS

Dogs have always rambled around our garden and before I caught the extreme form of the gardening bug, they posed no problem. Uncle Jacky's dogs never disturbed his gardening, but then they were two small, overweight terriers, inappropriately named Tiny and Topsy, who could hardly get out of their own way. So they caused no havoc. But Jacky had other challenges. It was only when I became converted to gardening that I appreciated how understanding he was of cats, dogs, hens – and indeed our children, who rode their bikes freely around his garden. I was far less tolerant and found it hard to keep my mouth shut when football-mad sons flattened roses and our two collies, who were then in residence, were tempted in the early morning to excavate the roots of shrubs planted the previous day.

Bran and Lady had come to us as two balls of black fur, who soon turned into leggy teenagers and finally sturdy collies. They were definitely a gardening challenge! Once, when I decided to mulch all the flower beds, a gardening sister suggested putting down an underlay of newspapers to improve the effectiveness of the mulch. It seemed a smart idea, but Bran and Lady had a smarter one, and decided that a morning newspaper would improve the quality of their life – so every morning the lawn was littered with shredded newspapers. Of the two, Bran was the less destructive, but Lady broke my heart. She had an irrepressible urge to sleep in a different tub of flowers every night. When confronted the morning after, and scolded for her misdemeanours, she would lie on the ground begging forgiveness and bury her face between her paws. She was the picture of sorrow and regret, but there was no purpose of amendment because the following night she committed the very same sin all over again. Yet, despite all her shortcomings, when old age finally caught up with her and she was laid to rest wrapped in a baby blanket, there were tears of sorrow as she was placed beside the other dogs in the doggy graveyard in the grove.

No replacements came after Bran and Lady, so for a few

years I revelled in a dog-free garden. Then my luck ran out as my dog-loving offspring, who were now no longer even resident, decided that home was not home without a dog. In favour of their argument was the fact that I was now on my own in a big, rambling house and garden, and they assured me that I needed doggy company as well as a guard dog. So began the hunt for a suitable canine companion.

I had only two specifications: it had to be a collie or a dobermann, because having had both breeds, I knew what to expect. We had all loved our collies, Lady and Bran, whose departure was deeply regretted. Also, years earlier, we had had Captain, a beautiful dobermann, and as smart as Einstein. Now, I am partial to smart dogs and have no tolerance for mutts; collies and dobermanns are almost human, I believe, though I am not so sure that that is any compliment to their canine intelligence. Captain had the stance of a well-bred racehorse and a docile temperament, but because the dobermann has such a bad image, people were extremely wary of him, even though he would not even growl. He never interfered with the garden, as rooting was beneath his dignity, and he carried out all his toilet activities out of sight in a discreet corner. He was the perfect dog – with only one big weakness: chocolate. He absolutely loved the stuff, especially Flake bars. If ever he found the back door of the shop open, he would sneak in quietly, and up along a side aisle to the sweet dump by the checkout, and there he would very daintily and unobtrusively pick up a Flake bar and make his way, calmly and unhurriedly, back out the door! One day a startled woman confronted me in amazement: 'Could I have imagined this?' she demanded, 'or did a huge dog come in just now and take a bar of chocolate?' That was quite a few years before Health and Safely took over – which was just as well because they would probably have closed us down. Anyway, Captain's weakness did not interfere at all with my gardening.

We went to the dogs' homes where the sight of so many abandoned dogs gave me a pain in my heart. We looked up ads in the Tuesday *Evening Echo*, which specialises in dogs, but there was still no decision reached about a replacement for Bran and Lady. Then one morning, when all was on the back burner if not forgotten, one son enquired: 'Is the dog idea abandoned?'

'I think so,' I told him.

'Ever think of looking in *Buy and Sell*?' he said.

'For a dog!' I exclaimed.

'They do everything,' he assured me, throwing a recent copy on the table as he left the house.

There, to my amazement, in *Buy and Sell* was an ad for two young dobermann dogs looking for a home as their owners were emigrating. These were of an age when they would be house trained, which was in their favour, as the last thing I was prepared to tackle was doggy training. I felt

I had done that quite often enough, thank you. Before I could have second thoughts, I picked up the phone and was answered by someone with a very posh English accent who informed me that he was located in Waterford and gave me his address – and mentioned a sum of money for his two charges that made me swallow twice. He must have heard it over the phone because he assured me that their blood lines were impeccable. Obviously, he was implying that you had to pay for blue blood.

Before I lost my nerve I rang a dog-loving son, who told me, without drawing breath, that he was on his way to me and that we were going straight to Waterford. I think he felt that it was best to catch this ball on the hop. So within an hour, Gearóid and I were on the road.

We arrived at a large lakeside house. Evidence of dog occupancy was immediately to be seen. On what one of my badly spoken friends call a 'F... off gate', which means an electronically controlled gate, there was a large sign: 'Beware the Dogs'. Having got through the first barrier, we approached a lesser one with another 'Beware the Dogs' sign, and on a third gate at a side entrance into what I assumed were the back regions of this well-guarded domain, was another such sign with the same proclamation. The presence of these dogs was very well heralded indeed, and even though I had not yet seen them I felt that they were a force to be reckoned with. Feeling slightly intimidated, we approached the front door, and it was opened by a dapper young Englishman, straight out of *To The Manor Born*.

We were led into an enormous bay-windowed room and our 'Tony Blair' disappeared into the rear regions to summon the two much-proclaimed dogs. They bounded in, and immediately took possession of a leather couch each. We were introduced to Kate and Lolly. They were sleek, black and demonic-looking, and put the hair standing on the back of my neck. Two pairs of piercing black eyes were focused steadily on us. They were, their owner informed us, two bitches, but not of the same litter and he produced a silver box full of papers which traced their ancestry back to Victorian times. No mongrel had ever sniffed around *their* gilded cages.

Coldly, they eyed us with disdain. We spent a few hours in the royal company, but it was obvious that these two ladies were not impressed and were deeply suspicious of our intentions. It was hard to blame them, because in comparison to their present circumstances they were certainly about to come down in the world. They were obviously two smart ladies who knew they had the perfect life and that we were up to no good.

When all the talking was over, their owner finally produced a blanket, which was obviously their travelling rug, and when they saw it they immediately followed it out to our car where it was placed on the back seat. They jumped

in on top of it. As far as they were concerned now, they were going places. It was decided that I should sit between them on the back seat – though it did enter my mind as we started off that, if they so decided, I could quickly become dog food. I badly needed the power of positive thinking as the two of them stood bolt upright on either side of me, looking straight out over Gearóid's shoulder, totally focused on the road ahead. Lolly, the smaller and less formidable of the two, slowly relaxed, but Kate was a hard coil of tension and stress, which erupted a few miles out the road in a stream of dog vomit on top of me! We came to a speedy halt and after a hasty, unsatisfactory clean-up, and ever mindful of the possibility of our two charges making a sudden dash for home, we continued on our way.

On our arrival in Innishannon we decided to drive into the yard and shut the gate before releasing our two passengers, who might, even now, make a bolt for freedom. They shot out of the car and around the yard and garden, full of alarm and curiosity. Then Kate went straight in the back door, through the kitchen and into the front room, where she promptly left a royal deposit on my cream-coloured carpet. She was, Gearóid informed me, marking her spot. Hopefully, I prayed, not an indication of things to come.

I rang my daughter, Lena, who, on hearing that instead of the anticipated one, we now had two dogs, was over the moon with delight and decided she was coming straight from work to be introduced. Then, visiting me at the time from Canada was my sister Ellen, and she too loved dogs. So Kate and Lolly were very warmly welcomed indeed. I seemed to be the only one with reservations about these two impressive ladies. That night we left them on the couch in the kitchen and during the night I got up a few times to check on them. I felt I was back on night feeds!

Lolly settled in quite quickly, but Kate still seemed restless and a bit edgy after a few days, so I rang my man with the Oxford accent to be informed that 'Kate is a one-owner dog and she has yet to decide to whom she will offer her allegiance, but once she has decided that, she will settle.' So we waited to see on whom Kate would confer her favours, and when it came my way I decided that it had more to do with food supply than royal patronage.

In the garden, some delicate plants met an untimely end and the lawn soon took on the appearance of Joseph's Amazing Technicolour Dreamcoat – bitch urine is not conducive to greener-than-green lawns. Another problem, though not of the gardening variety, also raised its head – sex. My two virginal ladies became the instant object of immense interest to the male village dogs. The news of their arrival went around the canine population of the village like wildfire. Dogs do not need to go clubbing and pubbing to meet members of the opposite sex – they kept constant vigil outside the gate, awaiting their chances. One mongrel, of varied and untraceable ancestry, was the leader of the pack. He was old, decrepit and hardly able to walk, and it was hard to know if he was capable of doing harm or if it was all in his head. Still, his vigilance was relentless and determined. But so was mine. He, however, had one big advantage over me in that he had only one thing on his mind. Every day the two girls were locked into the back porch when the gate was opened for deliveries to the shop; then the gate was locked and the girls let out. One day, however, the devious geriatric mongrel sneaked in the open gate, stole up into the garden and hid behind a bush. Unaware that he was lurking in the undergrowth, I locked the gate and let the dogs out. Later, I glanced out from an upstairs window into the garden and froze to the floor with horror when I saw who was frolicking around the lawn with Kate and Lolly. I raced down the stairs and chased him out the gate, hoping to do irreparable damage to some vital statistics. But had he done any damage? That was the big question. The thought of my beautiful, elegant Kate or Lolly producing mongrel offspring brought me out in a cold sweat.

The next step was the vet, to whom I explained the situation and who very reasonably pointed out that this was going to be an ongoing dilemma and that there was only one feasible alternative. The problem was that because of their impeccable lineage one of my sons felt that there should be at least one litter of royal pups. I, however, had no such

ambitions, as puppy delivery and night feeds were not high on my list of priorities. So I made a hasty decision that my two ladies would wither on their virgin stems, and I booked them in to the clinic – and began a cold war with Gearóid, who took a few weeks to thaw out.

But there was another problem about to unfold. The dogs had arrived in summer when the lawns were dry and hard enough to withstand their constant running; as the dobermann has greyhound genes, they are permanently running. But come winter, my smooth, velvet lawns turned into a ploughed field. One visiting friend stood in horror at the garden gate and gasped, 'What happened to your beautiful garden?' It took one word to account for the havoc: dogs. Another friend who did not like dogs informed me with relish, 'Always told you that dogs and gardening do not a good marriage make.'

I was determined to prove her wrong. But where to begin? Redesigning was the only answer to the problem. So I walked around and around my poor ploughed field, and thought and thought – and talked to my garden. I am a firm believer that a garden has a soul. Even though my velvet lawns were no more, maybe this garden had another, a different, future?

So I drew my plans, then redrew them, and even though I may be no Diarmuid Gavin a plan began to emerge. I showed it to a gardening friend.

'What? No lawn?' she protested. 'You can't have a garden without grass.'

'Who says?' I demanded.

'Well, anyone in their right mind,' she asserted.

In my plan the flower beds were going to extend out across where the lawns had been, and curving gravel paths would meander around the beds. I began to see that my plan had endless possibilities and got quite excited about it. But a garden on paper is one thing, and bringing it about in reality is quite another. Early every morning I was out in the garden with a spade, and all day I dug. I called it the Big Dig. Years before, I was visiting Lena in Boston, and the city was doing a huge transformation job, which they had christened the Big Dig. This was my Big Dig. It went on for weeks, and every night I crawled into bed, crippled and exhausted.

Dogs love company, of course, so Kate and Lolly really enjoyed the day-long togetherness. When the days were sunny, they rolled around in the dust, and when wet, they were covered in mud and their silken black coats became muddy brown raincoats. They had come a long way from the lakeside house with the paved paths and the 'F... off' gates. But they were loving it and were as happy as pigs in muck.

Slowly the transformation came about and my plan began to take shape. I carefully observed where the dogs ran and put my paths in that general direction. One neighbour told me, 'You know that you are gardening for two dogs' – and she

was right. But they were worth it! Kate and Lolly had settled in and by now their different personalities had emerged. Lolly was gentle, kind and self-effacing, while Kate was bossy, assertive and definitely the leader of the pack. Occasionally I had to remind her that that was actually *my* role.

Overcrowded beds were now thinned out, and plants that previously had had limited space could stretch their legs. I was beginning to enjoy this emerging transformation. When I went to the garden centre for additional planting, my priorities had changed drastically. Previously it had all been about soft blending of colour, but now it was about the survival of the fittest. Gone were the days of delicate, wispy elegance and in came the no-nonsense brigade. Kate was capable of chewing the head off delicate roses, so I learnt the trick of creating barriers of strategically placed tubs. Gardening with dogs was a learning curve and I was learning fast.

At first all the birds had taken flight with the arrival of Kate and Lolly, but then they realised that the dogs could not fly, and so they returned, but bird boxes had to be raised higher on the trees and the walls. Neighbouring cats, who had been constant visitors, now gave us a wide berth and the compost bins no longer had rodent visitors. And best of all, as the result of the arrival of Kate and Lolly I now have a far more interesting garden and have discovered that gardening with dogs is challenging but possible – and immensely enjoyable.

CHAPTER 7

THE FINAL CHORUS

September is a very indecisive month. It has one leg still in summer and the other reaching out into autumn. The gardener is caught in a dilemma between the two seasons. Do you cut the heads off the annuals and speed on their departure or do you continue dead-heading and watering, keeping them on an extended life-support machine? By now they are needy ladies, and without continued nurturing they will lie down and die. Their life is in your hands. So – decisions, decisions, decisions! The final decision usually comes down to the type of gardener you are. Are you one of the 'get to hell out of here' brigade or of the more tranquil 'let them be' fraternity?

Because I was born under the sign of Pisces, which is

represented as a fish swimming in both directions, I am like September: neither here nor there. But this year, as a result of reading an article by my gardening guru Charlie Wilkins, gardening columnist with the *Irish Examiner*, I am on a life-extending mission. Charlie proclaims that if you dead-head and water you can extend the life of your garden well into October. Now, that's a tempting prospect. Who would not want to extend this high note of perfection? The garden in September is at its most luxuriant. It glows more than any other time of the year. It's the great crescendo before the baton comes down for the grand finale.

The hydrangeas, like chorus girls, have flung their skirts in every direction and the begonias have thrown discretion to the winds and are tumbling around with total lack of restraint. Over the summer the brilliant geraniums have grown tall and muscular, and the nasturtiums are smothering all around them. In centre stage, stock and rudbeckia are giving an upright performance because this, after all, is their show time, and the rambling and climbing roses have lost their grip and are on their last, triumphant rampage, with bursting buds floating down all around them. Curving paths are becoming soft lanes of Fair Isle patterns. The dahlias are marching around the garden like Swiss Guards with the Bishop in his dashing red hat leading the charge, and the gladioli, like leaning towers, are tilting forward at precarious angles.

High above all these flamboyant ladies performing for their final ovation, the trees are daily changing their costumes to compete with the colourful chorus line beneath them. Trees are really the bone structure of the garden and all around them is the fleshing out of the bones. I married into a garden with mature trees, and that makes all the difference. If you have trees on site you have the structure of your garden up and running. Uncle Jacky's apple tree, with her great solid trunk and wonderful umbrella-spreading branches, is the heart of the garden. She is the venerable presence who, now in her second century, has acquired the wisdom of ages. The old seat beneath her issues a constant invitation. Who could resist such an invitation? And she does not disappoint. After a short time under her maternal, calming branches, the world is a better place. She slows you down and makes you think that maybe life could be taken at an easier pace. Her ancient roots connect you to the earth, and the tizzy you were in when you came in the gate drains away down into the garden soil. And as she siphons off the stress down your legs into the earth she gently calms your mind with her comforting presence and her leaves play a symphony of soft music above you. You are re-birthed into another world. The world of old trees. Could anything be more calming? When you look up into the branches of a great tree it tells you that the most wonderful and beautiful creations take time. An old apple tree is a multi-tasker. It purifies the air, feeds the birds, enhances the garden and provides food and comfort for us humans.

Beside the apple tree and sometimes intruding into her space is a Golden King holly. She is a real 'Johnny head in air' because at some stage she must have yearned for higher places and she transferred all her foliage to the top. Or did I, many years ago, with the arrogance of ignorance, prune off her lower branches in an effort to turn her into a long-legged model with plans of planting beneath her? I have forgotten now, and, in any case, her long, bare leg is a problem only at Christmastime when I have to bring a tottering step-ladder into the garden to reach her golden curls.

Uncle Jacky's planting was knowledgeable and far-seeing. Not so mine! A huge lime tree against the western ditch is testimony to my ignorance. At the time of planting we had beehives in the garden that have since moved on to the open fields. After reading in a beekeeping book that a lime tree is a great source of nectar for bees, a decision was made to supply them with a constant feast. On the day she was planted I discovered the absolute joy of digging and planting a tree.

The Honey Tree

The day was soft and mellow,
Growth was in the ground;
I went into the garden
Climbed to the honey sound,

Eased my spade through the fallen leaves

Of golden brown and red

And as I lifted out the earth

I made a soft brown bed.

Mother nature opened wide

Her arms of velvet brown

And on her maternal lap

I sat my young tree down.

All around her soft young roots

I folded mother earth

And when my baby tree stood tall

I felt joy as in a birth.

I tied her to a firm stake

To hold her in the sways,

A seasoned piece of older wood

To guard her growing days.

She came into the garden a light little slip of a thing, with no indication of the powerful woman she would become in later years, a bit like the slim brides you see in wedding photographs, who in later years grow into unrecognisable, sturdy women. But my lucky lime does not need to go on a diet because every couple of years the pruner trims her lower limbs to allow light in to the lesser beings beneath her and in the evening, when the setting sun glows through her

branches, she lights up the western side of the garden and you forgive her gigantic proportions.

But my next planting was a wiser choice and that resulted from a visit to the labour ward. What one views from the window of one's hospital bed can have a longterm effect. Your view, like looking through a camera lens, is restricted. In my lens, after having my first baby in the Bon Secours hospital in Cork, stood a grey, elegant little tree, with leaves that fluttered in the breeze. As soon as I got my legs under me, I made my way down to the garden armed with a record pad for baby feeds, and wrote down her name. She was a pittosporum Silver Queen.

Shortly afterwards I planted her inside the eastern wall of the garden, beside the gate leading out on to the road. There she flourished and grew into a mighty tree, providing a complete wall of privacy from the outside world. In a garden, if at all possible, it is lovely to be surrounded by walls of greenery. Trees create a green womb, insulating you from the outside world. As well as providing privacy and shelter, my pittosporum has many other blessings. She sends out the first scent of spring, which every year takes you by surprise.

On one of those bleak evenings that bridge winter and spring, you may be walking down the hill beside our house and suddenly you stop and sniff. The air is laden with the most heavenly scent and you think: My God, it's that time of year again – the pittosporum is doing its thing. And because she straddles the wall between the garden and the hill, she spreads her essence out over half the village. Thankfully, generous nature knows nothing about boundaries. The birds love her then as they sweep in and out in fluttering flocks, feasting on the little black berries that are all over her at that time of year. She is wonderful for flower arranging, and whenever I gather flowers in the garden the final call is always to her, as she enhances all arrangements with her unobtrusive, grey foliage.

The lime and pittosporum are the two big girls of the garden and, luckily enough, they are at opposite sides, and in between is a silver birch, which was a present to mark a silver wedding anniversary. To plant a tree for an absent friend is a lovely way to keep their memory alive, I think, and some-times I also re-christen trees in memory of friends.

On a few occasions, mistakes have been made that required drastic surgery. In my early days of gardening, I brought home a harmless-looking little green palm in a small pot, and when he had outgrown that I transferred him on to a tub, and finally – unwisely – into the earth. Then I discov-ered that there is no such thing as a 'miniature' palm. Give them leg-room and they do not know where to stop and will turn into monsters. This required the drastic action of enforced eviction.

But as you grow more selective, more elegant ladies will join you in the garden. From the top grove amongst dark greenery the cornus, in her wedding gown, waves down at me, and on a strategic corner the clematis Zara provides a veil that prevents an instant overview of the garden. An interesting garden, like a good story, unfolds as it goes along.

The acers are the gentle hostesses of the garden as with their delicate foliage they blend in and out between their more robust neighbours. They are the first to leaf in spring and the last to leave in autumn, and in between they provide a changing palette of colour, climaxing with a final display unmatched by any other tree. Their soft leaves turn to orange, amber and vermilion, and later embroider the earth around them.

But for sheer drama in the garden, there is nothing to match the golden frisia. Like all drama queens, she makes a late entry and, being temperamental, she could crack up with the slightest whip of wind. But give her the perfect location and she will glow like a golden sun and light up your life for the whole summer.

Now all the ballerinas line out in full regalia. Demure green ladies turn into scarlet women, demanding full attention, and even the sedate matrons of the garden cast aside their dark green cloaks and have a last vibrant fling before the show is over. This is the performance that they have prepared for since the first gentle flush of spring to the richer tones of summer, and now they have reached maturity and are ready to delight with the greatest show of the year.

CHAPTER 8

CRASH LANDING

The sycamore is a prolific lady and not always very selective about where she casts her abundant seeds. The female of any species, I realise, is not always the seed contributor in a union, and some species are even self-productive, or parthenogenetic. When I heard about this, I did an investigation. But my investigation wasn't caused by the sycamore, rather by a really dreadful intruder – the vine weevil. Plagued by this pest in my begonia pots, I decided to investigate its genealogy. I searched in a profound and weighty gardening tome produced by the Royal Horticultural Society to find out more about this monster whose progeny gorge themselves on corms, tubers and soft-rooted plants and leave them a shadow of their former selves. If you discover your once healthy geranium suddenly collapses as if struck by an unknown plague, in order to get to the root of the problem you must go to the root of your plant – and there you will usually find a tiny white maggot, offspring of the vine weevil, which is parthenogenetic. This is a one-sex unit in that he/she/it can self-produce without any outside assistance. But I digress! This is what constantly happens to me in gardening: I go into the garden to do one job and on the way fall over another one, and three hours later I remember what brought me in there in the first place. The sycamore!

Many, many years ago, long before my time, a sycamore seed arrived by bird carrier or was wind borne, and landed on our boundary ditch and got to work, and in jig time smothered the grove at the top of the garden. Over the years Uncle Jacky had looked at her and sighed with regret at her choice of location, but Jacky was not a tree cutter and neither am I, so the sycamore, grinning in delight at her spineless 'owners', spread herself with vigour, flinging around her rampant seeds. She was busy building up an extended dynasty. Every autumn I mercilessly set to work and tried to eradicate her progeny, but my demolition ability was no match for her high production rate.

My sister Phil, who is a serious gardener and takes no nonsense from unwelcome upstarts, looked at my towering bully whose toes were precariously curled into a stony

ditch and instructed: 'Get that to hell out of there before it comes down, bringing the Old Hall and you with it.' I agreed weakly, with no intention of doing as instructed. And so the sycamore and I lived unhappily together. On stormy nights as I curled up in bed, I worried about the possibility of her being up-ended and bringing all my garden plans and myself to a crashing conclusion.

A wise friend has often comfortingly assured me that worries are often overcome by events, and so it came to pass. One morning after a particularly stormy night, my sycamore tilted to a precarious angle, so the decision was taken out of my hands – isn't it great when a decision that you did not have the moral fibre to make is made for you!

So the tree executioner was summoned. Now, I dread the sound of a chainsaw – it brings mayhem to mind. When its shrill tones screech I can hear my father's voice echo down the years: 'It takes a tree a lifetime to grow and a fool can cut it down in five minutes.'

The executioners were armed with straps, ropes and swinging seats that bore them aloft like precarious bungee jumpers. They circled the sycamore like gliding hawks. Slowly she was stripped of her uppermost limbs that were borne earthwards like birds at a shoot, then fed into a mulcher that chewed them up and spewed them out into a waiting truck. My enormous sycamore was slowly turning into a slimline Twiggy and the garden was filling up with light – and then as her giant spine was gradually taken down, it was as if a curtain was drawn back and the whole sky suddenly appeared. I was filled with delight – and guilt.

That night I walked around the slain tree like a general after a war, but this general felt no glow of victory. There is something sad about a felled tree, like a great warrior after a battle. I tried counting her age and got lost after fifty rings, but then we are told that seventy is the new fifty, so maybe she was seventy. I sat on her wide trunk, running my hand over her giant sinews and wondering if Uncle Jacky was watching from his heavenly garden (as far as Jacky was concerned, it would not be heaven without a garden). Back the following day came the tree army bearing different gear, and the giant lengths were cut into circles and then, with a powerful, growling machine, finally split into a mountain of logs. The tree army departed and the logs and I were alone together.

Now, I love logs. I walked around them, sniffing their lovely, fresh timber smell, running my hand over them and feeling their lichened skin. The sycamore was no longer a threat that could crash-land and crush me, but had come down to my level and was my friend. We would have a warm winter together. But first they had to be wheelbarrowed down to the backyard and stacked in an orderly manner, and this job required more brawn than mine.

Every gardener needs a reliable Man for all Seasons. Sons

are wonderful, but every mother of sons knows all about 'Mom, I'll do that for you later.' 'Later', I have discovered, can be a long, long time! An instant and willing Man for all Seasons is the requirement and I am blessed to have a superb one. He is quick-witted, willing and a tireless worker.

He has, however, one big fault, and I found this out the hard way on his first visit. I had the misfortune to leave him alone with a pruner – a lot of damage can be wreaked in a short time by 'a tidier-upper' with a pruner. Coming back to a yard full of short back-and-sides and skinheads, I was transfixed with horror. Rambling roses with trailing locks had been shorn to the bone, full-busted shrubs transformed into anorexic beanpoles, and a towering black bamboo had shrunk to the size of a midget.

'What have you done?' I wailed, viewing the devastation.

'Yerra, they'll all grow again,' he blithely assured me.

From that day on, whenever Seasons is around, my pruner is never out of my sight and if I leave the garden even for a few minutes it is safely in my pocket. But apart from being a demon with a pruner, Seasons is the best, and he comes whenever a heavyweight job is on the agenda.

So, early on a fine autumn morning we began the long log draw. As he drew, I stacked. I love stacking logs; there's something very satisfying about it. The logs befriend each other and fit in easily together. As we progressed, I got a bit carried away, however, and decided to erect a rather tall barrier of logs to obliterate an unsightly wall. Up and up against the eyesore went the towering log wall, while I stood back at regular intervals to admire my skill and expertise.

'Are you sure you know what you're doing?' Seasons demanded as he upended another barrow of logs at my feet.

'Of course,' I assured him airily. 'I'm an expert at this.'

He eyed my great wall doubtfully. But I was full of confidence and glowed with satisfaction. This, I decided, was one of my undiscovered skills. Maybe I should have been a woodturner or a cabinet maker? Seasons disappeared up through the garden gate and just as I was about to place another log on my masterpiece, there was a sudden slide – I jumped back moments before the whole edifice collapsed forward onto the spot I had just vacated. My pride crashed beneath the logs as I gasped in relief at having escaped with two unbattered legs!

'What happened to the expert?' Seasons's head appeared through the hedge wearing a grin as wide as Kinsale harbour. I resisted flinging a log at him. 'Didn't I tell you that it should have been broader at the base?'

'You did,' I agreed, eating humble pie, and we began again with Seasons in charge.

'Watch the real expert at work now,' he instructed, stacking the logs with balance and precision, and as each log hugged the other, you knew instinctively that they were never going to part company. When the entire creation was in place you felt that it would be a pity to distort his beautiful pyramid by taking away even one log.

The previous winter, when the temperature had dipped to minus ten, my backyard had turned into a skating rink of black ice and I was glad to have a pile of logs just under the window of the back porch where I could reach out to help myself. Now, remembering this, we stacked the remainder of the logs along the wall under that window.

Though summer is gone, it is not yet cold enough to put down a fire, but just to look at the pile of logs in the back-yard makes me feel warm. There's something very comfort-ing about a stack of logs – their texture, colour and smell. Every time I pass them on my way to the garden, I smile. And my sycamore is on the way to reincarnation because, as ashes, she will return to the garden where she will enrich the compost of her former home. Nothing is ever lost in gardening. Now, if only I could convert those dreaded weevils into something useful!

CHAPTER 9

THE HOLLY TREE

It is 21 December, the shortest day of the year and I am actually sitting out in the garden having my lunch and being entertained by the antics of the birds as they flock to the feeders. They are the flowers of the winter garden, providing colour, activity and interest. It is amazingly mild for a mid-winter day, and the birds could well think that spring is here. It's hard to imagine that at this time a year ago the whole country was clung to the ground with black ice in minus ten degrees.

I lost all my cannas to that crippling cold of last winter. I was of the mistaken belief that there could not be killer-frost before Christmas. But I learnt otherwise! Not only did I lose my cannas, I also lost the pride and joy of my garden, a glorious tree fern. She had been a treasured gift in a large pot, which eventually she outgrew, and because she had over-wintered outside for many years I transplanted her into the garden. She was my special *protégé*! Placed strategically to catch the eye as you rounded the corner by the apple tree, she stood poised with the elegance of a ballerina and always brought visitors – and, indeed, sometimes myself – to a standstill in breathless admiration. She really was a beauty! As she grew taller with the years, her elegant stance conferred stature and drama on all her surroundings. She was my prima donna. But my beautiful ballerina crumpled in the crippling cold. Her long, quivering fingers collapsed in a sodden mess around her pirouetting toes. With her demise, that part of the garden lost much of its wow factor.

Then, at the Mallow flower show last summer I replaced her, but I had learnt my lesson. The replacement remains in its pot and, like the cannas, is tucked up safely in the back porch for winter. My father used to say 'experience keeps a dear school but a fool won't learn in any other.' How right he was. I have been educated. No more chances will be taken as the stress on my gardening peace of mind would not be good.

Putting the garden to bed is a late-autumn and early-winter undertaking, and has all the hallmarks of getting ready for winter visitors. But these visitors can be unkind: Jack Frost, high winds and sleety downpours. The garden

and the gardener have to be prepared for the onslaught.

In my early gardening days, I read an article by the garden-ing writer Helen Dillon, in which she wrote about observing the structure of your garden in winter. I remember thinking: what is she talking about, sure nobody in their right mind goes into the garden in winter. I had a lot to learn, didn't I? Now I love the winter garden and I also enjoy putting it to bed for the dormant season. It is now that the evergreen shrubs, overshadowed in summer by their colourful neigh-bours, come into their own. The rich colours and textures of their leaves glow in the winter sun that pours in through the bare limbs of leafless trees, now magnificent in their nudity. It is these evergreen statements that give the upright struc-ture to my winter garden. The garden is a different place in winter to the bustling brilliance of summer. It is resting, gone underground to recover and renew its vigour for the next major performance. To walk around here now is to be at peace and to learn that we too, like the garden, need time off-stage, time to recover in order to be ready to begin again.

This is also bulb-planting time. There's something very exciting about bulb planting – I love the delicate silken feel of the bulbs between my fingers and the knowledge that in spring they will burst up through the damp brown earth in a glorious riot of colour. This is the mystery of nature. I always intend to mark where I put down bulbs, and which bulbs went where, but as a gardener I am full of good intentions that never quite get realised. But this has its plus side because it later provides a spring full of unexpected surprises: I go around a corner and there under bare branches are snow-drops smiling up at me on a cold, miserable day. What a joy!

But before planting the spring bulbs, some of the summer tubers that have done their stint must be lifted. Now they are just clods of brown earth with no indication of their hidden potential. Removing as much earth as possible, I throw them into buckets. Some gardening experts recommend wash-ing them and others say no, so I wash one bucket and leave the other! In gardening, you have to find some things out for yourself by trial and error. But some advice is golden. At a gardening talk in mid-January a few years ago, Charlie Wilkins of the *Examiner* brought in a flowering branch cov-ered in tiny pink flowers that filled the room with a heavenly scent. He introduced us to Jacqueline Postill, a daphne that was then flowering in his garden. I had never seen or heard of her, but I recognised a treasure when I saw one – and cer-tainly when I smelt it. Flowering shrubs with such a scent are rare in a January garden. She would be a welcome addition because there is nothing that adds to the pleasure of a garden more than wonderful scents as you amble around.

In due course, I acquired a Jacqueline and placed her stra-tegically beyond the garden gate so that on entry she could wrap me, and my visitors, in her scented shawl. However, come winter, Jacqueline stood scentless and flowerless, and I thought: Charlie what were you waxing so eloquent about? But one evening the following winter, just before Christmas when I had forgotten all about Jacqueline, I went into the garden at dusk and a wonderful aroma stopped me dead in my tracks. Like a tracker dog, I sniffed my way to the source and there, along the branches of Jacqueline, were these tiny pink flowers wafting out their wonderful essence all over the garden. Thank you, Charlie, I breathed. What a gift from a generous expert. One of the many joys of gardening is that you can give and receive endless riches, free of charge. Now I have three Jacquelines and not only are they a winter blessing, but, for the rest of the year, elegant, upright evergreens.

I am not into hard landscaping, but I love odd-shaped stones and interesting pieces of driftwood and bog dale. When these old stones cover themselves with moss and lichen, they become little cameos of untold stories. In winter, the summer flowers that obscured the driftwood and bog dale have faded away and these ancient fossils reappear around the garden. The shapes of old pieces of bog dale stir the imagination and carry it along many unexplored avenues.

Over the years I have accumulated an odd assortment of pieces, bought mostly from a mountainy man who comes occasionally to the village with a van full of odd bits and pieces. He has a long beard and long hair, and the benign face of a Santa Claus. But this is no Santa Claus! After a long, protracted argument, an agreement on the price is reached.

The exchange has a touch of old-fashioned horse trading, which we both enjoy: there is no way that he expects to get the asking price, so he hikes it up to give himself manoeuvring space. Eventually he gets what he wants and I am thrilled with my old pieces of bog dale that settle into the rugged slopes of the garden. These wonderful, gnarled pieces came out of the ancient belly of the bogs of Ireland and they rest now amongst the craggy stones and old trees of Jacky's garden. You can sit on them, run your hands over their wonderful craggy texture or simply admire them. I absolutely love them.

Whereas there are many pieces of bog dale, there is just one piece of driftwood in my garden, but what a masterpiece! Originally washed up by the Atlantic into the mouth of the Féile river in Ballybunion, I came on her many years ago while out for an early-morning walk along the beach. Her arching, ashen branches protruded up out of the brown sand and swirling water of the beach. She brought me to a standstill, in awe at her beauty and possibilities. I tried to ease her out, but, full of seawater and hemmed in by wet sand, she would not budge. She was large, heavy and a long way from the boot of our car. I knew straight away that this project required male muscle. Unfortunately, my available male muscle at the time was of the juvenile, unwilling league, but collectively and with a willing father, all could hopefully be achieved. Have you ever tried to entice or cajole reluctant

teenagers to shift a heavy object that they deem useless? My beautiful driftwood was dragged along with contempt and accompanied by a wail of protest for miles of beach to the car. Under-breath comments about a crazy mother became more audible as the trek continued, and only the diplomacy of an indulgent husband kept my driftwood on course. I am never sure if tunnel vision is a curse or a blessing, but either way it is mine: I could see this beautiful piece gracing the garden and its endless possibilities clouded my brain and deafened me to filial protests. My determination rendered me hard of hearing and wordless, until eventually the car was reached. In the ensuing years, the sight of the driftwood would often trigger off a retelling of the humiliating escapade of bringing it home from Ballybunion.

My position was weakened by the fact that the previous year the team had undergone a similar experience with a huge rope that must have come off a large ship. It was coiled like a white whale along the same beach and I knew at first sight that it held endless possibilities! The sons, however, were blind to such anticipatory visualisation. But with coaxing, threats and bribery, the old rope was dragged along the beach back to the car, though progress was not accelerated by a tanned teenager of their own age enquiring sarcastically of my reluctant crew: 'Where's the boat, lads?' There's always one, isn't there?

For many years, now, the driftwood and rope have adorned

the garden, but while the rope has spent much of its land life simply draped around the handrail up the stone steps by the apple tree, the driftwood has had many reincarnations, chief among them being as the cave for the Christmas crib. With the approach of the holy season it is brought into the back porch to dry out so that the Baby Jesus, alongside all the other hazards of stable life, would not have the additional trauma of the Irish 'drop down' to contend with. In post-war poverty-stricken Ireland, the 'drop down' – from leaky thatch or broken slates too expensive to fix – was collected in discreetly placed buckets or chamber pots, and never publicly acknowledged. Nosy neighbours seldom knew if you had the dreaded 'drop down'. At least Jesus was lucky that in the Holy Land they did not have such a problem, but I still imagine my driftwood protection helps make him cosier.

So, come Christmas, the now-mellowed white driftwood takes pride of place on the hall table and its arching branches form a canopy over the homeless Holy Family. There they are joined by the traditional contingent of shepherds and sheep, but also by a large collection of birds and animals – it is my belief that this great occasion, rejected by the human world, was visited by flocks of birds and by many from the animal kingdom. So my crib is the home of geese, swans, robins, camels and many more little creatures collected over the years or given to me as gifts by friends. I love arranging this extended crib as it involves the unwrapping of many much-loved objects, and when they are all in place it is full of memories. Uncle Jacky and Aunty Peg's ancient crib figures mingle with ours, which results in a doubling up of babies and mothers – but in today's world, I tell myself, maybe back-up is needed to cope with all the extra pressures. Some figures are showing the wear and tear of the years, with a legless shepherd here and a headless Wise Man there, so extra personnel are required in other departments to distract the eye. But despite the many handicaps of my characters, doing the crib is always a joyful occasion and when all are in place it is time for the holly and ivy.

Every Christmas, as I cut his holly, I say 'Thank you' to Uncle Jacky. What a blessing his holly trees are now. The planting of a holly tree is a gift to future generations, and so I inherited a great gift. Maybe, on acquiring a garden, the first tree planted should be a holly – as they are slow growers it will take time before you reap what you sow. Over the years I have planted others, so now I have a variety of holly trees, and one thing I have learned is that they do not like to be disturbed. One baby tree began life in a tub and then got planted at the wrong end of the garden, but when I righted this wrong and shifted her, there were sulks and tantrums. She threw off all her leaves and stood naked and sullen for months, but I did not give up on her and fed, watered and coaxed her, and in the end she relented and decided to forgive me and put on her coat and get on with the business

of living. Now she is a tall, silver-haired dame, standing to attention beside the red door of the Old Hall.

One of the best bits of gardening advice I have read came from Brian Cross, one of the gardening experts of Cork, who advised pruning your holly trees at Christmas, which, fortunately, is the correct time to do it, and thus at the same time providing baskets of holly for decorating. It gives double satisfaction to collecting the holly, relieving the guilt of stealing the wonderful green branches, and when I stand at the garden gate each Christmas and look back at my newly shorn trees, I say: 'Thank you, Brian.'

On the farm where I grew up a big clean-up of the stables, stalls and yards always took place before Christmas, and to this day I carry on the tradition with a big clean-up of my backyard and garden. My Man for All Seasons comes to help, and he is the best tidier-upper I have ever met. He goes into every corner, and together we create a spotless yard and beautifully tidy garden. This year we shifted another holly tree that was in the wrong place – her neighbouring tree had grown too large and was crowding her out, and she was also being overshadowed by a taller sister holly. At the other side of the garden she would have her own space to make a statement. Gardening is all about shifting, balancing and creating scenes that are easy on the eye – though the plants must cooperate, of course! The earth was in beautiful condition for moving her, as severe frost or heavy rain had not yet come, so we eased her out, gently embedded in a huge clod of soft earth, and sat her into a waiting bed, then tucked her in with rich brown earth and garden compost. Hopefully she would not even realise she had been moved. Most plants, like people, if moved at the right time and into more pleasant surroundings, will put up with the disturbance.

Late on Christmas Eve, it is wonderfully peaceful to wander around the garden and check up on all the friends. It is a starry night tonight as I walk slowly around, and the street lamps from the hill outside cast a muted light over the stone wall, allowing me to meander easily along the paths. I tread gently under the Golden King in case of disturbing the two doves. The little holly tree that we just moved seems to be happy in her new home. The two Wise Men are sheltering under the trees, while St Joseph is keeping a fatherly eye on everything. It is Christmas in the garden.

CHAPTER 10

SNOWDROPS AND TULIPS

J anuary was never my favourite month but once I began to write, paint, and garden it became my most creative. Now, once Christmas has packed its bags and departed, I stack a pile of logs beside the fire and hibernate to write and to peruse glossy garden magazines.

Through the window I can see the vibrant colours of my window boxes smiling in at me. Is there anything more rewarding than spring window boxes? They generously begin to kick into life in January, and while the world around them is grey, black, brown and bereft of colour, they glow with brilliant life. Dragged down in early winter from the top of the garden where they over-summer, they are placed on the front window sills looking sad and forlorn. But after loving doses of feed and water they begin the greatest comeback in the history of the plant world. The dehydrated and forlorn primulas begin to sit up and take notice, and come late January they are strutting their stuff on the sills along the front of the house. They glow with the most gorgeous colours – yellow, mad orange, deep purple, bright red and royal blue. They shout at passersby: Look at me, look at me! They certainly do not believe in hiding their light under a bushel, but are a real in-your-face job, precisely what is needed on a grey January day. Then up through their greenery come the snowdrops, crocuses, miniature daffodils and tulips, striving to outdo them. They all dance together in a riot of colour. One can only rejoice in their delight. The perfect harbingers of spring! Come a dry hour I go outside to feed and water them – after all, if we had to survive solely within the confines of our own bed we too would need constant sustenance.

On a mild day I escape out the back door and meander around the garden – thinking, planning, imagining, examining. My daphne Jacqueline Postill pours her wonderful scent around me and the self-effacing sarcococca wafts little clouds of essence through the air. All about are buried treasures waiting to come to the surface. Some of them are just beginning to peep up. The wonderful hellebores are already there, making a statement, and their twinkling

white bell-like flowers are winking from beneath the green glossy leaves. The daffodils are coming through and assuring me: We are coming, don't worry, spring is on the horizon – hang in there. But the most delicate of them all – the brave little snowdrops – have stolen up through the challenging conditions and formed a white chorus line in hidden corners beneath sheltering trees. Because of their delicacy, the snowdrop brings out the maternal in us gardeners. Like newborn babies, they seem too fragile to face the rigours of our world, and unfortunately in my garden they have the additional hazard of Kate and Lolly, so they are reserved for untrodden ways. Due to my canine friends I can never become a fullscale snowdrop gardener, but I love to admire them in other people's gardens.

So when my friend Maura rang in the dying days of January and asked, 'Would you like to visit an open garden?', I jumped at the chance. 'An open garden at this time of year!' I gasped. 'That must be a brave gardener.'

To me, other people's gardens are like a brewery to an alcoholic and, where gardens are concerned, I have no shame in me. I peep in through gates and peer around hedges and become a real Kitty the Hare (if you never heard of her, ask your grandparents). The wonders that other gardeners achieve are a constant enticement to me to attain better things at home. And I love the people who visit gardens. All united by a common bond, total strangers avidly discuss their worms and compare the merits of horse dung versus dung of the poultry variety. My gardening guru, Charlie Wilkins, writes that we who visit other people's gardens do so to steal – but before you succumb to the vision of old ladies furtively ducking out through garden gates with plastic bags full of uprooted plants, perish the thought! We are an honourable fraternity. Charlie finishes that statement by adding 'ideas'. Because new gardening ideas are what we are all after. I have an intolerant friend who once informed me, icily, that there is nothing more boring than other people's grandchildren, and she was probably right – but the direct opposite is true of gardens because there is nothing more fascinating than other people's gardens.

So it was with bated breath and unbridled enthusiasm that I arrived at this open January garden, which was in suburbia. This house was built in pre-Celtic Tiger Ireland before builders shrank gardens to postage-stamp allotments. Built twenty years ago, this house had a decent-sized garden back and front. We Irish, whose ancestors came from open spaces, were never meant to graze on priest-collar strips. But that is what has happened to us. Not so, at this particular house. This woman had a fine stretch of land around her home, enough to fan the spirit and heal the soul of any city dweller. And here the gardener had put every square inch of her piece of holy ground to work. I stood at the gate, glued to the ground with amazement. This was gardening at its very

best. It was not yet spring, and here was a garden alive with variety and contrast. Snowdrops, hellebores, daffodils and endless others that I was not informed enough to identify. A warm fur coat of rich dark brown mulch hugged them all, and needless to mention, there was not a weed or piece of debris in sight. Above them, still-naked acers and strategically placed grasses and shrubs proclaimed good planning and design. It was absolutely breathtaking. I crawled along like a beaver, head down, gazing at the ground below me, absorbing every last detail.

Now, to me a snowdrop is a snowdrop is a snowdrop. Not so to this woman. Here was an array and diversity of breeds that boggled my mind. We were in the presence of a connoisseur and when she smilingly informed me that last summer she had visited my garden, I cringed. But gardeners are a tolerant and understanding lot, and not a one-size-fits-all crowd. We come in all shapes, sizes, ages, understanding and knowledge, with one common denominator – love of the job. I lay no claim to being an expert gardener; I am a digger and a doer who never ceases to be amazed at the wonders that unfold around my ignorance, so the thought of this knowledgeable woman feasting her eyes on my confusion of a garden did cause me to wince a little.

It was obvious that this lady, as well as being a wonderful gardener, had a deep love affair with snowdrops. Arranged in in every available corner were rows of little pots, each sprouting a different variety of these pristine white, delicate, drooping angels of the spring garden. I did not even attempt to try to remember the unpronounceable names that proclaimed the identity of each one of these beauties – that was way out of my league. I was satisfied simply to absorb their beauty. I am of the belief that in order to enjoy the birdsong you do not necessarily need to know the name of the bird. That's my feeble excuse for my gross ignorance in certain fields of gardening.

However, on a garden walkabout you learn a lot. All gardeners love to share their knowledge – present one of them with an ignoramus and they love to wax eloquent. You will be filled in on all the do's and the don'ts, and you will be blinded by expertise. I understand this perfectly well because give me someone who is less well informed than I am (and they are there) I love to hold forth like a gardening expert and I get carried away with the desire to impress. Or maybe this scenario could be viewed in a more kindly light – could it be that gardeners get such enjoyment in their chosen hobby that they want to go around converting the populace and enticing all to gardening bliss?

Inside this garden gate was a map of years of knowledgeable gardening. Around the back were three well designed homemade wooden compost bins with hinged covers, underneath which was compost in varying conditions of decay (yes, I looked! – nothing excites a gardener more than a smelly compost bin). This was the crème de la crème of garden compost. I decided that floating around here somewhere had to be a handy husband, and, sure enough, soon afterwards I identified him as the strong, fit-looking man who was viewing this visiting crowd with a benevolent eye. The same crowd are not into high fashion but believe in warm boots and weatherproof rain gear, so come what may they are prepared. These are not a fine-weather team. A shower runs off them like water off a duck. And they were here in great numbers. A cold wet day was no deterrent to their enthusiasm. My friend, Maura, who is new to garden visiting, said in surprise as we viewed the crowds, 'I thought that there would be very few here as the forecast was so bad.' She had a lot to learn about garden visitors. We are a hardy breed. Later, as we drove home, she asked would I be interested in visiting the Altamont garden in Carlow that specialises in snowdrops? Would I what! We planned it for two weeks' time.

❦ ❦ ❦

Today we were having what my mother used to term 'a pet day'. In the midst of a series of deluging winter days came this beautiful soft spring day with unbroken sunshine hour after hour. People passed by my door with a new pep in their step. What a difference the weather can make to our sense of well being. Stimulated by the great day, I whipped the sheets off my bed and later, for the first time in months, hung them out to dry in the garden. I love to see washing blowing on a clothes line. As I pegged the clothes along the line I did a temperature check and decided that it was a day to have lunch in the garden. Kate and Lolly thought that all their birthdays had come together when I sailed out with a tray, a sight that they had not seen for a long time. Dogs love company and they could be forgiven for thinking that summer had arrived.

As I sat there in the sunshine I watched the birds queue up at the feeders. It had not been a harsh winter, and yet the birds were starving. They flocked around the feeders and there were many that I could not identify. Had a lot of refugees flown in? I loved to watch them feed and jostle for feeding space and I knew they would later fill the garden with their singing. In the bird world there is a set time for everything. They may not be biblical scholars but they practise the bible creed: there is a set time to eat and a set time to sing. Birds pay for their keep in song.

It was invigorating to be eating outside for the first time this year. The garden looked good – dog-trodden, yes, but good. I knew that because spring is a temperamental lady we might have many miserable days up ahead, but this one day was a gift to keep us going. You really cannot segregate the seasons by the calendar because nature does not always adhere to the rules.

Spring came today
Breathing softness in the air
Opening gates within my head.
The birds felt his presence
Pouring forth symphonies
Of unrestrained welcome.
It was late January
And he just came
To have a peep
Trailing behind him
Along the valley
Wisps of purple veils.

❦ ❦ ❦

Yesterday was our day for the Altamont garden. I sometimes find that on these occasions my preconceived picture of a place such as Altamont is totally at odds with the reality I encounter. This place surpassed all expectations. As soon as we went in the gate, we stepped back into an enchanting, restful world of an earlier era. The old house, whose previous occupants ranged from landed gentry to nuns to monks, finally came into the caring hands of Corona North, who dedicated her life, as her father had, to the enhancement of the gardens. On her death, she left the estate to the care of the Irish state, which proved to be a wise decision because

now it is in the hands of loving experts. Our state may get many things wrong, but thankfully they came good in Altamont. The wonderful old house is now unoccupied but not abandoned, and will hopefully one day be restored to its former elegance. It sits like a grand, faded old dame in the midst of her treasured gardens. Draped in a shawl of climbers, including a one-hundred-and-fifty-year-old wisteria, she is the queen of this domain, quietly resting and giving a heart to the flowing gardens and woodlands all around her, and looking down over a beautiful lake where swans and ducks perform for her entertainment.

This beautiful garden is both formal and informal, ranging from free-flowing woodland to hidden corners of formal perfection. You meander along – and I mean meander because there is in Altamont an all-pervading atmosphere that calms the mind and induces a sense of tranquility. Wonderful old stone walls draped with trailing climbers meet you as you round unexpected corners. But it is the trees that are the jewels in the crown. As you explore the wonderland of snowdrops around their gnarled roots, these ancient centurions form a steady, protective canopy overhead. This is a paradise for the well informed horticultural enthusiast, but even for the less knowledgeable it is a delightful and invigorating experience.

To bring home plant remembrances of the day, we visited their plant sales area and had a wonderful hour being tempted by many beauties glowing with good health and horticultural expertise. There I met a lady driving a trolley laden down with plants. 'You have a few days' work in that trolley,' I remarked. 'A few days of joy,' she corrected, smiling with delight. 'Spring is my doorway into days of delight.' She had said it all!

Chapter 11

Flushed with Pride

The toilet in the back corridor always gave the first signal that trouble was brewing. When it backed up and refused to function as it should, it sent out red-alert warnings, emitting the language and aromas of the underworld: all was not well in the underbelly of the backyard. Down there were bedded ancient clay sewerage pipes that were well past their sell-by date, and in recent years only kept doing what they were supposed to do by constant monitoring and a gruelling colonoscopy – sticking strong, plastic piping down their throats to free their clogged innards. This was a back-breaking, disgusting job, and when I sensed that it was on the agenda my blood pressure went up by several degrees. With years of practice I had become an expert on U-bends and water force, but sometimes it took hours of huffing and puffing from the upright, to the kneeling, to the prone position, to finally achieve the ideal angle to make these ancient pipes clear their clogged bowels. Afterwards, there could be a free run for many years before another blockage would occur, and I would be lulled into a false sense of security that all was well in the lower regions of my backyard.

But then the problem would again rear its ugly head. Sometimes, if the downstairs toilet failed to ring the alarm bell, it fell to a shore in the backyard to send out the distress signals. By then the problem was much worse, and the pipes far more congested. An able-bodied son had to be summoned to lift off the ancient, solid iron manhole cover that weighed a tonne. And if no son was available, the son of a good neighbour would be kidnapped off the street! It is one of the perks of village living that help is never too far away.

A blocked sewer in summer is an unwelcome visitor, but in winter it is a nightmare, leading to hours of cold torture. After one of these episodes, opinions were voiced: something will have to be done about those sewerage pipes in the backyard. These statements were always accompanied by an accusatory look in my direction. I was the stumbling block to that 'something' being done, because, as one non-gardening son acidly proclaimed: 'We don't have a backyard out there,

we have a jungle.' Therein lay the problem. How could I clear out my over-planted backyard so that the whole place could be dug up and re-piped? Impossible! For years I had dodged the issue, but deep in my own body system I knew that sooner or later the day of reckoning would come. And come it did. What accelerated its progress was the arrival into the backyard of a heavy machine to assist in the re-roofing of the house. This machine was a step too weighty for my archaic sewerage pipes, and they finally decided to collapse beneath it and die. They sent out the usual distress signals and I assembled my tools of counter-attack, but I discovered I was fighting a losing battle. My underground pipes had finally called it a day and I faced a total shut-down of the entire underground system.

We who freely flush with pride owe a huge debt of gratitude to Thomas Crapper – now, who is he, you may well ask. Well, he is the man who invented the flush toilet that we all take so much for granted, and he also designed the London sewerage system. His name, of course, holds his story. I heard about Mr Crapper after I wrote my book *Quench the Lamp*, which included a chapter named 'The Royal Wee' about my experience of the transition from the po to the flush toilet. At that stage, though availing of his facilities, I had never heard of him, but while I was doing a book signing in London, a very dapper and charming man congratulated me on my delicate handling of an indelicate subject and handed me a beautifully illustrated little book called *Flushed with Pride, The Story of Thomas Crapper*. Hence my knowledge of the said gentleman. Over my years of struggling with my underground sewerage pipes I developed an affinity with Mr Crapper. Now, he and I were again going to share an experience because the day of applying his expertise was finally here. It was time for action, no matter how undesirable.

Prior to the big excavation, there would have to be the big clear-out. Where to start? My mind boggled at the prospect. The first thing I needed in my corner was an understanding plumber-cum-builder-cum-jack-of-all-trades, but, most of all, a man who understood the strange mind of a gardener. Charlie was my man. His wife is a gardener and a flower arranger, so he is well versed in the idiosyncrasies of us green slaves and understands how our minds work: when he came into my backyard he would not think he was dealing with a crazy woman. And so it was. Calm and serene, he looked over my 'jungle' with a non-judgemental and unperturbed gaze, for which I was very appreciative. 'We'll have to pull back a few things,' he gently informed me. 'Probably,' I agreed, deciding to play it his way – but behind the calm exterior my head was whirling with plans of how best to approach the big shift. I am a firm believer in the boy scout motto 'be prepared', so when a critical son joined us and announced, 'Yerra, Charlie, we'll throw those old things sideways when you start,' I decided on the need to have all my ducks in a

row prior to the commencement date.

But before that deadline a big decision had to be made: to slab or not to slab, that was the question! In anticipation of this dilemma, I had gone around to various garden centres and stone yards and viewed thousands of paving slabs, and every time came home in a state of total confusion. I am a ditherer by nature – it takes me a long time to figure things out and make up my mind – but in my defence, I must say that when I do finally make a decision, having viewed all the options, I can make a very good decision. At least, I think so! In our family we call this thinking/dithering the 'What do you think, missy?' process. The term was introduced by a sister of mine who worked in the radiology department of a large hospital where an eccentric doctor who, when he wanted to introduce a new system, went around to all the staff whose names he could never remember and que-ried each one of them in turn: 'What do you think, missy?' When all were consulted, he made his own decision. When I began this line of approach, one smart son promptly told me: 'Why bother asking us? You'll do exactly what you like in the end, anyway.' I went to great pains to explain that having consulted all, a wiser decision would be reached. He was not impressed. 'You're like the government with their fecking white papers,' he informed me. So much for my consultative process!

But I was determined to do my homework and having

looked at and debated on the merits of cobblestones, natural stone and crazy paving, I was on the verge of going crazy myself. It's amazing how total application to one singular problem can turn that problem into a mountain in the mind. But the problem shrank when Charlie arrived with a treacherous looking circular saw to mark out the prescribed area to be replaced. After a quick, assessing look, he applied his saw, and in a cloud of dust cut out an oblong patch all along the backyard, leaving an undisturbed headland around the sides. As he straightened up I asked him, 'Charlie, what would you put down there?'

He thought for a while before answering; Charlie is a man for considered opinions. 'Maybe concrete again?' he pronounced, nodding his head wisely.

'I don't like fresh concrete,' I protested.

''Twon't be always fresh,' he reminded me philosophically, 'and, sure, with all these plants and pots you won't be seeing too much of it anyway.'

So the decision was made. Charlie had hit the nail on the head and, besides, my backyard could never be considered a posh suburban patio lending itself to streamlined paving, but, as one of my garden visitors had stated, was more like a haggard. It had a rugged look, so maybe paving, however well chosen, would not blend in with the old concrete. There were other contributory factors that favoured this decision: as the old concrete would remain untouched along its edges, all the largest containers that stood by the walls could be left in place. What an ease that was. Along there was Aunty Peg's old bath tub, now the home for a Warm Welcome climbing rose and shrubs of various hues and denominations, and another old bath tub that came from I'm not sure where, but now host to a huge *Melianthus major* and an assortment of other bits and pieces. There were also two redundant water tanks filled with plants. It was great that they would all remain untouched.

Even so, there was still a huge amount of shifting to be done. 'When will you begin the dig out?' I asked Charlie. 'Early tomorrow morning,' I was told, and I knew that Charlie's 'early' meant the crack of dawn. So the time for the big shift had come. I summoned my Man for All Seasons. Now, sons fit the bill for certain jobs, but they have their drawbacks in that they always think they know better than their mothers, and you finish up with things done not exactly as you would want them. One time I found a postcard in a bookshop of a smug-looking female and the slogan beneath read: I'm not bossy, I just have better ideas. I knew exactly what that meant! So, Seasons it was. Prior to his arrival I had worked out exactly where everything was to go and with a hand truck belonging to the shop, and with brawn and a certain amount of brain, the two of us gradually got the yard evacuated up into the garden and around the edges. As it was early February and real growth had yet to begin, only bare arms stretched out from the pots and containers. The plants were still enjoying their winter 'sleep-over', so the process reminded me of moving sleeping babies without waking them up. In full bloom the pots would have presented a much more cumbersome removal problem.

But some of the old containers resisted strongly and groaned in protest. One ancient wheelbarrow, with its rusted wheel that had not made a turn for years, refused point-blank to budge. Seasons and I had to lift and drag it up the yard, its rusted hinges growling in anger. The large clay pots were easier – they could be tilted sideways without disturbing their occupants and rolled along like whiskey barrels in an old brewery. The whiskey barrels themselves, into which I had planted slips of trees in moments of tree madness and which had now caught up with me as they spread their arms wide, could happily remain safely parked where they were. If I had decided on paving that would have been impossible and I shuddered to think of the consequences. Even as it was, it took a certain amount of ducking and dodging to avoid being decapitated or blinded by stark, bare branches protruding from moving containers.

'You're a glutton for punishment,' Seasons told me cheerily as he whipped pots in all directions. He is the ideal man for such a job and can transform chaos into law and order in no time. Kate and Lolly darted back and forth between the pots, wondering what on earth was going on, but delighted

with all this sudden activity in their domain. They were unaware that for the next few days a stop would be put to their
gallop in the restraining confines of the back porch.

The following morning I awoke to the sound of breaking concrete. Charlie's son, Ivor, was in action with a mini-
digger. He was tossing cracked slabs of old concrete into a
trailer, which regularly disappeared out the gate in a cloud
of dust. Luckily the local football field was absorbing filling
at the time in the creation of a new car park, so our disposal
problem was solved by a few quick spins up the village. Soon
my backyard was reduced to an oblong sunken well. The
back gate was open, with Kate and Lolly safely locked up,
so an inquisitive neighbour felt it was okay to venture in to
see what was going on. 'Are you digging a slurry pit, Alice?'
he enquired smartly. 'Would you like to be buried in one!' I
retorted. It had been hard work; I was in no mood for jokes.

After a few hours the work was done and strong new pipes
straddled the yard. So the back gate was locked and Kate and
Lolly let loose. Normally, when they are turned loose, they
race up the yard in a contest to be the first through the
narrow garden gate. Now they peered down in amazement
at this new development and wondered what on earth had
become of their yard. Slowly, Lolly eased herself down into
this new, unknown space, criss-crossed with spanking new
orange pipes, and found her way up the other side. Kate,
older and wiser, picked her way around the edges and joined

her buddy at the garden gate. I wondered how they would cope with the experience of being locked up during the upcoming concrete pour.

Of course, with our Irish climate, there was no way that such a job could be done without the usual baptism of a downpour. So, true to form, work ground to a halt while rain battered down for two days and turned the backyard into a mud bath, which Kate and Lolly thoroughly enjoyed; they came in each night with muddy socks, making the kitchen an extension of the backyard.

But at last a watery sun decided to have a brief look down on us, so we availed of the precious time and the concrete-mixing truck backed in the gate. Her shiny spout poured out what looked like masses of concrete into the sunken cavern. Katy and Lolly stared out through the glass of the back door, curious about these further strange goings on. The truck finally pulled away and Charlie and another son of his, Brian, began the great levelling off. It was easy to see that this was Charlie's forte and the trowel whipped back and forth in magnificent sweeps, transforming uneven lumps of concrete into smooth perfection. All was going according to plan.

I withdrew to the kitchen and was just about to put on the kettle when a thunderous roar of rage rent the air. I bolted for the back door thinking that some disastrous catastrophe had taken place. It had! Kate had managed to prise the door open and was lodged knee-deep in Charlie's perfect concrete.

Lolly was close behind her, similarly immersed. The usually calm Charlie was beside himself. I was afraid to move lest I join the two fools of dogs embedded in the concrete. Charlie, however, quickly recovered his equilibrium and with one swift swoop, like a giant forklift, he landed Kate into the back porch, with Lolly in quick succession. 'Wash those two bloody fools fast,' he instructed, 'or they'll get hard paw.'

Rather than washing, I felt like thumping the two of them. But common sense prevailed and they were soon knee-deep in suds. Dobermanns are big dogs who don't take kindly to foot baths, but because they are also highly intelligent and they sensed that they had in some way breached a certain code of ethics, they were all of a sudden very compliant and obliging, lifting their paws obediently into the bucket of water. They then retreated to their baskets by the Aga and, like chastised children, rested their heads on their paws, cocking an occasional speculative glance in my direction to ascertain if they had done sufficient penance to atone for their misdemeanour.

That night the yard was cordoned off, and Kate and Lolly had to be led out the side door of the house and taken around the footpath and in the back gate for a run around the garden. This continued into the following day, until it was safe for them to walk on the concrete. I breathed a sigh of relief when they could once again bolt straight out the back door and tear up the backyard into the garden as if they were competing in a greyhound race.

It was time for the big return. Give any gardener a clear space and their designing instinct will instantly spring into action. It was now safe, I decided, to wheel out the delicate greenery that had over-wintered in the back porch. After two terrible winters, during which I had lost many delicate plants that had been my pride and joy, I had taken no chances and brought indoors all my fragile beauties who might succumb in minus ten. But a mild winter had come instead, so it was now time for them to step out and take their place on my new, white-faced concrete yard. Into pride of place went my wonderful tree fern, who stood waving her bronze arms, but I knew that with a little bit of love and care new green shoots would soon unfurl. She was to be the centrepiece, and all around her Seasons and I gathered the chorus of other pots, pans and wobbling wheelbarrows. When all were in position, as Charlie had told me, there was very little of the new concrete visible. Over the following weeks rain poured down and within months my white concrete had turned green and become native; just as Charlie had predicted, it didn't stay fresh-looking for very long. My backyard began to look like its old self – and I could now flush with pride too. Thank you, Mr Crapper!

CHAPTER 12

STRUGGLING!

I was suffering from post-'flu inertia. As I kicked myself reluctantly around the garden, words of my mother's echoed back through the years – encouraging words, which would come forth when we reluctantly undertook a challenging but worthwhile project. She would say, thoughtfully: 'Isn't it great that we have the mind on us to do it.' She meant it. Her statement contained all the determination and wisdom of a lifetime bravely eking out a livelihood on a mountainy North Cork farm during the harsh mid-decades of the last century. I pondered on it this mid-March day as I walked around my garden carrying a bucket of self-pity and weighed down in a cloak of post-'flu inertia. I did not have the mind on me to do anything. I needed a good kick in the backside to get going.

The 'flu hit like a ten-tonne truck and blew me off my tracks. A contributory factor could be that I had spent the previous few weeks working madly in the house and garden as if there was no tomorrow, as well as planning an upcoming village event, with no brakes on. Ignoring the flashing red lights of headaches and stiff joints signalling oncoming danger, I hit the Stop sign in full flight. Some people heed no warning signs and tear on until they hit the wall. Then they wonder in dismay: how did that happen? I am one of these not very smart people. I blamed the weather, which was mild and sunny: February and March had no business behaving like June. Even the roses were fooled into beginning to bud. But one of my 'I told you so' friends laid the blame firmly on my own shoulders, informing me acidly: 'You have a vintage engine and you were going like a new model.' There was no answer to that, so I kept my mouth shut.

Now, after the crash, I was picking up the pieces, not sure that they were all still in working order; it wasn't very comforting to know that if there were any damaged parts there was no one to blame but myself. At least I had the consolation that the garden, unlike myself, did not need attention and had benefited from the huge spurt I had put on in February. The debris of winter had been cleared away, dead limbs chopped off and stalks from last year's perennials removed.

My Man for All Seasons and I had emptied a compost bin

and used up all the lovely compost that had been maturing for two full years and was absolutely alive with worms. These worms had done a great job and all the kitchen waste had been digested into soft, rich compost. Worms are wonderful – and our native worms are tough enough to digest Irish rubbish! I have three compost bins with no bottoms, which means that the worms can come up out of the earth and take possession, and I give them plenty of time to do their recycling. There is great satisfaction in lifting up the cover of a compost bin to find strings of squirming worms clinging to the edges. Sometimes I gingerly catch these curling strings and throw them back into the dark depths of the bin, with instruction to get back to work. A compost bin in the garden is like a pot of gold – better, actually, because you put in rubbish and get out brown gold. No better deal than that, with double the return on your investment. The stock exchange couldn't hold a candle to it. As well as that, you reduce your bin charges because all your household waste disappears into the cavernous depths of this smelly, self-absorbing monster. My bins are camouflaged and concealed in the depths of a sweet-smelling *Viburnum tinus*. These three bins are my silent, hidden garden slaves, undercover agents within which thousands of worms work non-stop on my behalf. I adore them.

Now the worms were the only workers in the garden as the gardener herself had come to a standstill. I realised that I had burnt out my engine, so it was time to sit down and watch the birds feeding and wait for my soul to catch up. Sitting-down time in the garden is a rare luxury: as soon as gardeners sit, they see jobs demanding attention. But for once I did not care. I needed nurturing time. Kate and Lolly are much smarter than their owner, I mused: they stretch out and relax in the sun every time an opportunity arises.

During my working blitz, I had planted begonia tubers in the summer window boxes in anticipation of sunny days ahead. They were now lined up inside the windows and it was intriguing to go around and watch the tiny shoots begin to emerge out of those dry, crumpled tubers. When you put these unpromising-looking, wizened warts into the moist earth, you really have to trust that the miracle of nature will change them totally and bring them to exotic, colourful life.

Whenever you take time to sit and gaze in the garden it is amazing the wonders you witness. The upright yellow tulips were waving to me from behind the bronze ferns, who had yet to put on their new shawls. These were all sheltering beneath the little weeping acer, who had bravely donned her new finery before hesitant summer peeped in the garden gate. Every year, at the first hint of better days, out comes the acer, full of the joys of spring. What a delight she is, dancing into the garden in her bright green skirt while everything around her is still shrouded in sombre grey. The early arrivals in the garden are the most stimulating of all. Other selective ladies wait until the house is full before they make their

A garden should be in a constant state of fluid change, expansion, experiment, adventure; above all it should be an inquisitive, loving but self-critical journey, on the part of its owner.

The 'feral' blue bells are just coming out by St Joseph's. The garden is full of birds and they are so busy. There was a lovely cream bird with a red cap at the feeder yesterday. Never saw one of them before. How do people live without a garden? This place enriches my life. Probably could not write without it. There are so many birds in and out of the stones in the old hall. It is like a high rise hotel!

April 2nd Sat 2.30pm '05

What a gorgeous day! Lena is home, came last night and is in form. She will be here for a few weeks and it will be so good. The clothes line is of towels as a result of the feast getting Goo's house. They were great. Left the house this morning for 3 weeks in August from the Hughes. So will work out O.K. Should really do a bit of gardening but feeling lazy. All is well.

grand entrance, and even though they are all welcome at any time of the year, the first arrivals are the heart-warmers of the gardening year. This is probably why we all love the snowdrops, crocuses and daffodils who assure us that winter is almost gone and there are better days ahead.

During those dormant days, when my energy levels had plummeted, I sank into a sitting and absorbing mode. Usually when I sit in the garden, it is from sheer exhaustion, but now I was content to just be still and do nothing. When you do this, you are much more receptive to the wonders around you. I have an expert gardening sister who has often told me that the times that you sit in the garden doing nothing are often the most productive. Now I knew exactly what she meant. I have often been so busy out here that I have failed to notice anything at all.

I brought out my garden diary from the back porch. It has never been taken into the house as it is only for garden writing. A present from my husband, Gabriel, many years ago, it has brought me endless joy. It records feelings and images, not facts. It is a 'how am I feeling' and 'how is my world' journal. Usually it is filled in on sunny days when I am in harmony with my surroundings; such moments are transient and need to be captured like beautiful butterflies in the memory box.

Now I saw that when you are at odds with the world the garden puts its arms around you and hugs you closer. You simply sit and let the garden take over your being and massage your wounded spirit. And when you begin to feel at ease with yourself, you can write, and then go into the house and bring out a tray of tea. There is no gourmet restaurant in the world to compare with the ambience of eating in a much-loved garden. Your garden loves you back one hundredfold. It is a priceless investment in your sense of well being. Soon I feel that I will be on the move again.

CHAPTER 13

THE GARDEN SHED

I n recent times the humble garden shed has somehow become the bolt-hole of the 'menopausal' or retired male. They have evicted the humble gardener and transformed the shed into an upmarket hobby haven, with activities ranging from setting up model railways to wine making – plus, these sheds also function as male confession boxes. Nothing to do with gardening at all! How did this happen? Gardeners were in first and surely had squatter's rights. Are the non-gardening fraternity, who have never discovered garden therapy, seeking the solace of the garden without getting their hands dirty? Do their computerised souls yearn for communion with their origins, and their endings – in the earth? At the end of life what finer conclusion could a person reach than as compost from which a great tree might spring? Are these new 'shedders' expressing a deep-rooted longing for the earth – could any of us ask for better than to be reincarnated into a tree? But no matter what purpose our garden shed serves, it is still a wonderful friend, and as these humble places become grander and more high-tech, I fondly remember Uncle Jacky's garden shed.

Uncle Jacky's shed was used for sprouting his early seed potatoes and to hang his bulging strings of pale onions from the rafters as they seasoned to golden amber. He would have been astounded to hear the buzz of a toy train speeding around his sacks of spuds! As for wine, the nearest he ever came to the smell of alcohol was when Aunty Peg poured *poitín* into the Christmas pudding. Uncle Jacky's garden shed had neither plumbing nor lighting, and smelt of damp earth, Jeyes Fluid, and contentment. In there he stored his old wooden wheelbarrow and a limited number of garden tools, which on wet days he repaired and fitted with new handles. Through the cobweb-laden rafters was threaded his curved scythe that he used occasionally to clear the totally wild area at the top of the garden when he could not trace wily hens who had decided to hatch out of sight on summer days. A tar barrel stood beside the door to capture the rainwater off the galvanised roof – this door of many colours was Aunty Peg's decision-making zone on her various colour schemes for her kitchen over the years, and with time the colours

had blended into the impression of a kind of hazy peren-
nial border: Aunt Peg had unwittingly been an impressionist
artist!

The door did not quite make it to the floor, so the inner
sanctum of the shed was accessible to Jacky's dogs and cats,
who availed of it on wet days. The stone-cobbled floor sloped
towards the door, so in the event of a downpour penetrating
the roof, the water had easy access to the exit. On wet days
the rain beat a muffled tempo on the roof in rhythm with
the regular drips into the tin buckets that were strategically
placed to catch the musical dropdowns.

Internal activities were confined to dry areas. This shed
could never be described as luxurious, but it enshrined the
spirit of its aesthetically attuned owner. He had built it himself with odd sheets of galvanised and rafters left over after
the additions to the back of the old house. Over the years
it became shrouded in ivy, rambling roses and an assortment
of wild climbers, and had blended itself completely into its
background. From the outside it gave the appearance of a
mound of greenery with its 'wild-flower' door. On enter-
ing, it took a few seconds for your eyes to grow accustomed
to the shadowy interior, and then, slowly, muted shades of
browns and greys welcomed you into this cave-like structure,
with the old stone garden wall as its gable end.

On hot summer days when Uncle Jacky worked up a sweat
digging in the garden, he would step into its cool interior to

rest on an old seat that was the bottom half of a kitchen chair evicted from Aunty Peg's department. A jute bag filled with straw was its overhanging cushion. On this he sat to cut his *sciolláns* (the bit of the potato with the sprout for planting), tossing the *sciollógs* (the bit without the sprout) into the hens' bucket and wearing a coarse bag across his lap to catch the earthy debris which he then scattered to the waiting hens. This stool was also his resting place and you would sometimes surprise him silently saying the rosary as the beads slipped slowly between his fingers. It was his meditation hut, as the natural feng shui in there was conducive to contemplation. Years ago, when I had a houseful of demanding teenagers and hungry guests, I sometimes hid in there too and sat quietly to regain my equilibrium. I privately christened it 'The Hermitage'.

Jacky's garden bench was an old door straddled across two timber barrels and beneath it, neatly stacked, were his sprouting boxes and some old iron buckets for use around the garden. Above the bench his tools hung off a row of rusty nails, and stacked in the corner were his spade, shovel, rake and pike. This little shed told the story of the man who owned it. Every handle was moulded into the shape of his hand and each well-used tool lovingly cared for and cleaned. He had a limited number of tools, with nothing surplus to requirements. His well-worn leather gardening boots hung by the laces from a hook off the low rafter. One year a robin

built her nest and raised a family in one boot, so a retired pair had to be retrieved from a cobweb-clad butterbox under the table, and the nesting boot became an annual family home and delivery ward. A little holy-water font hung beside the door and Jacky never passed it without taking its blessing with him out into his garden.

Uncle Jacky escaped daily from the demands of his village shop out into this little bit of heaven. Though loved by all his customers, he was too saintly a being to be engaged in any type of business and in an ideal world would have enjoyed life in the hermitage of Skellig Michael, isolated far out to sea off the Kerry coast. His garden shed was his private Skellig, and when its occupant finally stepped into the great unknown, the shed returned to the natural world. On the beautiful warm, sunny August morning when he winged away from his little earthly heaven to the greater one to which all his paths had led during his life, his garden was filled with white butterflies that fluttered around this little hermitage. From this base he had cultivated his garden that fed us all and was home to a meandering flock of hens and countless birds. He was not into pruning back, so everything flowered and flowed with free abandon and birds had a multiplicity of choices for their building sites. A lawnmower was not numbered among his requirements, as his grass was kept in check by hens, cats, dogs and later by our children riding bikes around it. He did not have a lawn as such, and maybe what he had could best be described as a wild-flower meadow – with the emphasis on 'wild'. Slips and cuttings were exchanged with gardening friends, and when they visited, a long, meandering garden walk was always on the menu, during which the merits of different breeds of spuds, cabbage and garden fruit were discussed and analysed.

Afterwards, Aunty Peg – if she approved of the said visitors – served them tea under the old apple tree. Aunty Peg believed in the language of the teapot and I always knew that if visitors did not get the 'tea in the garden' treatment they were not numbered amongst her chosen people. Jacky always smiled indulgently at this and never inquired why some of her previous recipients had fallen from grace.

Even though Uncle Jacky's shed is long gone, its simplicity sometimes springs to mind when I view the confusion that abides in my own shed. He never choked his with miscellaneous clutter. Mine is a cauldron of garden tools discarded as too old, too heavy, or simply pure bad purchases. It is stuffed with my mistakes. I have four spades, three of them not quite fitting the bill. One is short, with a cracked, unrepaired handle, and the next one I purchased was made of steel to avoid such calamities, but proved too weighty – thence on to another short model! For years I bent down over this short-handled spade until one day a visiting farming friend demanded, 'Why the hell are you breaking your back with that short little bastard of a spade?' 'But that's what is in all the garden centres,' I protested. 'Oh for God's sake, woman,' he exclaimed, 'you were reared on a farm. Did you ever see your father use a yoke like that?'

That evening a spanking new long-handled garden spade appeared over my gate. And I never looked back. Why, you may well ask, did I not dispose of the others? The answer to that is the 'that might come in handy some day' syndrome. Or maybe I am expecting to shrink into a miniature version of myself with the passing years! The same thing happened with my assorted collection of shovels and rakes. So now if a tribe of lost Lilliputians arrives in Innishannon I can sort them out with perfectly suitable garden tools. In the meantime, my wonderful collection of tools fills up one corner of my groaning garden shed and they usually collapse sideways in an unruly heap when I search around them to retrieve balls of garden twine that invariably roll between them.

This is my second garden shed. The first one rotted in location; its spine sagged and the floor collapsed beneath me until it was finally declared a danger to human occupation and finished up in the back of a skip. That skip was a wonderful opportunity to get rid of countless other bit and bobs — but no, they all sneaked back in under the guise of the possibility of 'one day being just the thing to have in an emergency'. But, at

least, the purchase of the new shed afforded a golden chance to sort things out and this time I availed of the opportunity of putting shelves in the new model. For one whole month I had absolute law and order in my shed, and everything was visible and accessible – and I wondered how on earth I had tolerated the former confusion. I was living with perfection and I loved it. But, unfortunately, there is a theory that an empty space inevitably fills itself, and I proved that theory correct. When a home-decorating outbreak had spun itself out, a variety of paint cans filled the shelves, along with wobbling paint trays and brushes soaking in jampots of turpentine. They were meant to have been washed out and put away when the exhaustion of the painting epidemic had evaporated. But by then that exhaustion had been replaced by another of equal proportions due to some cause now lost in the mist of fading memory. Then, gradually, the turpentine evaporated and the paint hardened – and thereby hangs a tale. It was the end of my lovely order.

Above the multi-coloured jars hangs another tale in the form of a picnic kettle that in its day was a wonderful acquisition for the prevention of forest fires while picnicking with an unruly brood. The brood has now departed, but the picnic kettle lingers on. Also lurking in the shadows is a collection of tools belonging to the mother of a non-gardening friend who felt good that her recently departed mother's tools had found a sympathetic home. How could I tell her that her mother's saw would not now cut a cobweb and that the pruner was pure useless? Sometimes being honest is just too cruel, and so my garden shed unwittingly became a contributory factor in bereavement therapy. It has also become the receptacle for the forgotten dreams of football champions whose helmets and hurleys lie gathering dust in its depths. Parts of the bikes of potential racing champions are also tucked in behind the staking sticks for staggering gladioli. And though my lawns are now a thing of the past, bags of grass seed still stand in a corner. A fishing rod of a once-budding angler is woven across the spindly rafters, while bags of all kinds of everything, including a variety of garden ties, hang from the ceiling. Monty Don would not use all these ties that I feel are necessary to have at the ready, and when I view his garden potting-shed with its orderly rows of budding pots, I wonder if there are rows of TV garden slaves lurking off-camera who maintain all this law and order. I bet there are. Of course, I am only looking for excuses for my own disorder because I know full well that Uncle Jacky had no garden slaves to maintain his haven of order and tranquility. Some day – maybe some day – I too might achieve the order and peacefulness of his wonderful hermitage. I can always dream!

Friendship IS THE MOST PRECIOUS *flower* OF ALL

CHAPTER 14

TEA IN THE GARDEN

I love June. The very word itself rolls off the tongue like cream off the back of a spoon. Because it is book-ended by May and July, you feel secure that you are really in the depths of summer. Now the full summer cast is on stage and any blemishes in the bones of the structure are hidden by the flowing gowns of the leading ladies. Summer is all-forgiving. Just like the young who, no matter what they don, look good, so the garden, now in the full flush of its vigour, breathes health and beauty. An early-morning walkabout is an invitation to dance with enthusiasm through this energising, vibrant world. Come high noon, rather than lunching in the sunlit area inside the high stone wall, I seek the cool solace beneath the sheltering umbrella of Jacky's apple tree.

She stretches her maternal arms out over half the garden and provides a green haven beneath which I love to sit and watch the action all around me.

On first viewing, a garden may appear to be a quiet space, but when you sit silently in its heart you see its veins pulsing all around you. Once the birds feel that you have disappeared into the landscape they come back into action. The robin is the least inhibited of them, and when he has deemed that you are not a threat he will join you soon after your arrival. If you come out to dig the garden, he is there in moments to see what marvels you might uncover. The blackbird is similarly curious, but far more reluctant to come forward, and the thrush is the most reclusive of all of them. I love the blackbirds, but when I see them bully the thrush I feel like taking up arms in defence of the shyer bird. But with nature it is best not to intrude and I have never forgotten the words of my father: 'If we upset the balance of nature we pay a terrible price.' Admittedly, he was referring to pollution and tree felling, but it probably applies right across the board. It is one of the reasons that I am a reluctant weedkiller sprayer as, like antibiotics, I reckon that if they kill the bad guys they cannot be clever enough to preserve the good guys in their elimination process.

In high summer it is a case of glorying in the whole wonder and miracle of nature. I sit in the midst of a riot of colour, my garden a display of uncontrolled exuberance.

Now, I love the concept of an all-white, peaceful garden and sometimes dream of treading elegantly through drifts of snow-white perennials beneath bowers of delicately trailing *Madame Alfred Carrière*. When I visited Sissinghurst and viewed the wonderful white garden of Vita Sackville-West, I sighed with envy. But, regretfully, not for me the restraint of Sackville-West, though I can still dream of that unattainable tranquil white retreat.

Our deepest emotions are very much interwoven into our gardens, I believe, and sometimes they can surprise us. Dreams of the future and memories of the past prevail, and the smells of a childhood garden are never forgotten. I have a friend who has a corner of her garden dedicated to snowdrops in memory of a beloved mother who loved snowdrops, and who died when my friend was very young. The spirit of her mother is enshrined in those snowdrops, and there in her beloved garden her mother is always with her.

There is no end to the wonderful healing processes that can take place in a garden. A garden can soothe the bereaved and calm troubled minds that have endured all kinds of trauma. The summer garden warms the cold bones of grief and poultices the mental wounds of the stricken. Walking into the summer garden is walking into the arms of a loving friend who hugs away all your cares. You may come in the gate bothered by the world outside, but herein is peace, calm and tranquility.

Summer is the high point of the garden's annual perfor-mance. Though I am one of those fools who think that the current season is always the best, there is no denying that there are very few experiences better than tea in the garden on a summer's day. It is when all your efforts are rewarded and you can sit like a queen and admire your surrounding kingdom. So if you are not a gardener, you are depriving yourself of one of the most deeply satisfying experiences of life. I am a late convert to the joys of gardening and like all converts I am over-enthusiastic in my crusade for conver-sions. I am a born-again gardener! So forgive me if I wax over-enthusiastic. Now I will get off my soap box ...

It is only in recent years that I have stumbled into the wonderful world of flower festivals. Most of these seem to take place in summer – and in churches. If you want to see flower power in action, these are the places to go. Here, amazing gardeners crack into exuberant overdrive and bring the world outside inside. These are creative geniuses in full flight. They recre-ate historic, biblical and imaginative scenes and unbelievable arte-facts with the power of flowers. Sometimes the festival has a theme and gardeners play out the scenes in wonderful depic-tions, and a story is told as you walk

from exhibit to exhibit. These scenes take hours of painstaking creation and while all is being assembled the church is alive with greenery, the sound of snipping pruners and an occasional few words not in the Lord's Prayer.

Then, come the opening hour, all debris is eradicated, perfection is achieved and peace prevails. To walk around now is to experience the magical achievement of nature combined with artistic skill, and the magnificent architecture of churches in which this activity usually takes place is a fitting backdrop for all the wonderful design.

When I come home from one of these shows I am all fired up with enthusiasm and full of delight at the wonders I have seen and I just love to go out into my own garden and let the magic of creation seep into my soul. Late on a summer's evening, the choice of location is inside the high stone wall that faces west. The sinking sun filters through the trees on the western ditch and highlights the glowing tips of the flowers and shrubs around the garden. This is a ballet spectacular, and drifting birds and butterflies provide fluttering movement. The blackbird is giving his last performance of the day. Sometimes, making a late appearance, my two white doves wing in and disappear into the Golden King, ignoring the nearby dovecote made specially for them – like a lot of older residents, when provided with a new home they refused to move.

At this time of evening in the summer garden it is

soothing to sit late and watch dusk drift into darkness, and then the street lamps on the village hill outside the wall turn the garden into a world of shadows. My grandmother, much to my amusement at the time, used to pray that she be protected from a sudden exit from this world; the direct opposite would be my choice of departure – the best would be sitting in my garden sipping wine on a summer evening. It would be winging from one heaven to another.

CHAPTER 15

RETURNING

I abandoned my garden for a whole week. No self-respecting gardener would do that in summer. It is a breach of all good gardening rules. I broke the rules and paid the price.

But, oh, the joy of coming back. To walk out into a yard and garden glowing with colour. There is no doubt but absence makes the heart grow fonder, and now that I have returned I am full of delight just walking around and soaking it all in. Though I did abandon my beloved garden, I had taken precautionary steps. Before leaving, I had fed and watered everything to the hilt. I had told them all to behave themselves in my absence. But there was a silent enemy watching and listening, and just waiting for me to turn my back. Hundreds of slugs, with their ears cocked, live permanently in the high stone wall that lines the eastern side of my garden. They hide there, always waiting to catch me out. Snails too. Everywhere! Millions of them.

Now, not believing their luck, they saw their chance. On my departure they moved their entire encampment out of the wall into the battlefield. They were an army on the move. In for the big kill! They munched their way through countless plants. In their total ecstasy snails even abandoned their homes between the plants. Healthy hostas were savaged until they were reduced to drooping net curtains. It is unbelievable the havoc unrestrained slugs can wreak in one short week. Normally I counter-attack on a daily basis with grapefruit skins full of beer, in which they drown themselves and create a clammy mess that I dump in the compost bin with great satisfaction. Or I carefully place slug pellets where the birds and dogs cannot reach them, or protect my plants with an environmentally friendly spray. But rain renders all these efforts inept and, after heavy showers, the slugs smell victory and begin to muster their troops, so you have to keep on the attack and be ready with your weapons at all times. It had rained heavily in my absence, so all my advance protection methods were rendered ineffective. The slugs saw the green light. They swept across the garden like an invading army into an abandoned battlefield, leaving countless victims strewn behind them. I almost cried when I saw my hostas – their main course – but they also had my dahlias as

a starter, and finished off with my petunias for dessert. They gorged themselves to obesity, and though I am not a murderer by nature I collected every visible overweight culprit and jumped on them with delight! But the harm was done and my revenge did nothing to repair the damage.

The slow road to resuscitation began. Working with a scissors, I carefully cut away all the perforated leaves of the poor hostas and dahlias, leaving them a shadow of their former selves, but in gardening you sometimes have to be brutal, and nature has a wonderful way of restoring itself. The petunias, however, were another story as the slugs had ravaged them right back to the bare stems, so there was no answer to this destruction but a total cut back to base, with the dubious hope that they might somehow reinvent themselves.

The valiant roses simply required de-heading. Once their redundant hats are removed, roses will soon don another, but if you leave the old tattered one in place they seem to think that a fresh new one is surplus to requirements. So a brisk de-heading is the answer, and I have the perfect tool for this — a little gadget called, of course, a 'de-header', acquired at Mallow flower show for a few euro. It's magic! A pruner, of course, is capable of doing the job too, but not with the same skill and simplicity. It is such a simple solution that on first sighting this little device I doubted its effectiveness, but because the woman who was selling it sold only well-researched, top-class garden offers, I took her advice on trust.

'Where did you see this?' I asked her out of curiosity. 'Chelsea,' she told me. Enough said. We Irish do many things well, but when it comes to gardening we have to hand it to the Brits. So I nipped around my roses with this tiny little gadget that was definitely designed by a gardening genius.

Even in the case of a week's abandonment, you will pretty much get away with neglecting most things growing in the earth, but not so plants in pots or window boxes – and if you are one of these lunatic gardeners, as I am, with the habit of planting hanging baskets, you really are asking for trouble by leaving them to their own devices in summer. However, all is not lost if you have put your trust in begonias, because they are flowers for all seasons, and, come burning heat or relentless rain, they seem to be able to withstand the pressures, which means everything in our Irish climate. So my hanging baskets, though a bit forlorn, had survived pretty well and after a good watering and nurturing feed, they perked up and looked much better. I felt like a doctor doing the rounds and administering the right medicine for my patients. I had once read a book by a woman on the therapy of watering flowers (therapy for the waterer, you understand): it makes one feel like a redeemer, she proclaimed.

My cannas, however, were not so tolerant of neglect because, being in pots, they had both slugs *and* thirst to contend with, which seemed a bit too much for them. They stood silently in forlorn tatters, infusing me with guilt. First

I attacked the slugs, then administered the scissors treatment, and finally doled out a sustaining feeding and watering. After a few days they were sitting up and taking notice.

The sweet peas were not so forgiving though, because they are extremely thirsty and need to be picked regularly or they will decide the show is over and go to seed. They were teetering on the edge of that decision, and had to be coaxed back into action with profuse watering, plenty of feeding and a lot of cajoling. Gradually they recovered, but demanded so much attention that I swore never again to disappear in summer as they never quite regained their former glory. Sweet peas are the ballerinas of the garden world and, like everything delicate and beautiful, they require constant care. They are a bit like ourselves in that they need to be needed. They reward you, of course. When you take the scissors and nip their delicate, fragile stems they twine themselves gently around your fingers like gossamer silk, and their wonderful fragrance wafts up your nose like a heady wine. They decorate the house in the most wonderful way; they do not appreciate upright, rigid containers, but relax better in old, wide-mouthed china jugs where they tilt over the edge in profusion and turn your kitchen into a fragrant perfumery and a picture of perfection. When a jugful of them graces your kitchen table, you will feel like waltzing around the kitchen. What a wonderful gift.

CHAPTER 16

GETTING READY

Oh lord of little things
Look down upon our labours,
Just to make our garden
A little better than our neighbour's.

'Will you open your garden this summer for the Tidy Towns?' he asked calmly. Fundraising for the Tidy Towns competition is an annual event in our village.

'Holy God!' I demanded. 'Have you any idea how much hard work goes into the preparation of a garden for opening to the public?'

'Not a clue,' my non-gardening friend assured me blithely.

'Brutal work,' I informed him sharply, and even though I

knew it was a pointless exercise I elaborated before he could say anything. 'Do you realise that if you intend to open your garden in the summer you have to start thinking about it the previous autumn?'

It was his turn be dumbfounded. His face registered a look of total amazement and disbelief. 'But isn't your garden grand the way it is?' he said with the assurance of someone who doesn't know one end of a garden spade from the other.

'You're clueless,' I assured him.

'I know,' he grinned. 'Not into this gardening crack at all. But we need money to pay for those history signs around the village and your garden is a dead cert to make a few bob. And those history signs were mostly your big idea anyway.'

He had me there. I was beginning to feel fenced in, and that there might be only one response to this dilemma.

'Think about it,' he instructed and sailed out the garden gate as if he was Alan Titchmarsh having given instructions to a whole host of garden slaves. The problem was that there was only one slave in this garden!

But he had sown a seed, and like most seeds it began to take root. Now, it wasn't as if I had not done this before. I had. And enjoyed every minute of it once the garden gate was open. The problem lay in the months prior to the opening. Opening your garden, in one way, is a bit like going into the labour ward: once the pains are over, you enjoy the fruits of your labour, but you never quite forget those labour pains

either. Time may dull the intensity of them, but the memory lingers on in the back pages of your mind. That, however, does not prevent most people making a return journey! The same applies to garden openings. So I knew in my heart that I was going to open my garden even though there was not a lot of time in gardening terms to get ready.

Then the doubts began. People had seen this garden before – would they think it worth their while to come again? They had seen it twice, actually, as it had been opened twice as a fund-raiser for the local church – and had brought in a size-able amount. The amazing thing about that experience was that most of my fellow members on the fund-raising com-mittee thought of it as a soft money-maker. One of them even told me that it was 'money for jam'. I kept my opinion to myself, which is not my usual form. For those previous openings, my garden had had curving lawns and delicate plants. It was truly a thing of beauty and a joy forever. At least, that's my memory of it, though sometimes memory lends enchantment to the view, of course.

Now, two dobermann dogs and four years later, all had changed, changed utterly, but, unlike Yeats, I knew that a terrible beauty had not been born. Then I got a brainwave. Surely out there in the gardening world there were people wrestling with the problem of gardening with dogs? I had my theme! Could I combine garden enthusiasts with dog lovers? Would that work? Time would tell, but I'd give it a try.

Inside the garden gate the hard work was about to begin. I whipped off my rose-coloured spectacles and walked around the garden, viewing it like a surgeon assessing a patient for major surgery. This garden was about to go under the knife – or the pruner, to be exact. Kate and Lolly accompanied me on my journey of inspection, delighted with all this sudden walking back and forth and delving around and behind trees and shrubs. I looked askance at hidden places that for months had been used solely as the dogs' exercise territory, evidence of which lay around in abandoned bones and the wrapping from items they had stolen from the back shed behind the shop. All this would have to stop. People did not come to open gardens to view abandoned bones and boxes. My two dogs were about to get a crash course in good behaviour. They needed the discipline of TV dog-training expert Caesar in their lives. I would instil his great sense of discipline in these two. And yet another cloud was about to darken their horizon: dog kennels. They'd had this experience once before when they were evicted for a family wedding: my daughter had decided that her elegant friends, swaying around on top of eight-inch heels, should not be torpedoed by exuberant canines. Another possible problem had been that if inquisitive guests decided to investigate hidden corners they might emerge with shoes scented with 'Dobermann Mystique'; their new aroma would definitely challenge the wonder of 'because you're worth it' perfume.

So the two dogs were evicted the day before the wedding for a night in the kennels. And they did not like it one bit. They were not happy campers! When we returned to collect them they were delirious with joy and almost dragged the arms off us as they pulled us by their leads to the recovery van. They shot in the home gate and circled the yard at top speed, over twenty times at least, to make sure that all was well with their home place. They were a picture of dancing delight. And, like abandoned babies, they would not let me out of their sight for weeks afterwards. Could I put them through this ordeal again? That was the big question.

Before that decision had to be made, there were a lot of other things to be done: namely a total overhaul of the whole garden. Whenever I face that undertaking, my plan of campaign always is to start at the right of the garden gate and from there on it's a case of 'head down, backside to the wind and keep going' until I get around the whole garden and back again to the other side of the gate.

So I collected my little kneeling pad that I had acquired at the Mallow flower show and my well worn trowel and faithful pruner, and got going. Suitable and user-friendly tools are a prerequisite to enjoyable gardening. Over the years you develop a working relationship with your garden tools and gradually they cease to be tools and become close working companions. The handles smoothen into the shape of your hand, and my kneeling pad now moulds itself around my knees. It is bright red so that when I get called away and later come back not quite sure where it is, its bright colour flags me to the right spot. Another part of my essential garden gear is my well-worn garden apron, a present from a very practical sister. It is ample and all-encompassing, with deep, deep pockets, capable of holding all sorts of everything.

So thus garbed and equipped, I was ready for action and took to my knees. Slowly but surely, law and order was introduced and the pile of weeds in my garden hold-all mounted up. This hold-all is also bright red, and I have punctured holes in it so that if I abandon it overnight and the rain comes, it does not fill up and pull the arms out of me the following morning. Now it was overflowing with weeds and I decided that it was time to empty it – and therein lay the first problem. My back had grown accustomed to being at right angles to my hips and now decided that maybe that was a preferable position to being upright, and so the slow easing of the hinges began and I thought of the wise man who wished for a hinged back for gardening. With much huffing and puffing and many encouraging licks from Lolly, which impeded rather than helped progress, I was finally upright. Gardening is a killer on the back. And as for 'hands beautiful' – forget it! I normally don gardening gloves, but sometimes I get carried away with enthusiasm and they are forgotten – and hours later I look down at the hands of a cave woman. I dragged the hold-all up to the grove at the top of the garden where

I upended it on to the compost heap. Then it was back to work.

For several weeks I crawled into bed each night on all fours, doubting my ability to rise again the following morning. But rise I did, and slowly my body became accustomed to changing gears from the horizontal to the perpendicular, and my back hinges grew more supple. And so it went on, day after day, until finally I was back at the left-hand side of the gate. Every evening, on completion of the day's work, I would view my achievement and feel a glow of satisfaction, and now on the final evening my sense of elation could surely be compared with Sir Edmund Hillary's on conquering Mount Everest.

On completion of my task, I decided to treat myself to a body massage to say thank you to my abused anatomy, so I rang my friend Pippa and booked myself in. As she assisted me on to her massage table, she demanded, 'What the hell have you been doing to yourself?' 'The garden,' I told her meekly. 'There is a place called Stop,' she said sharply. But there was nothing sharp about her soothing hands as she massaged warm oil over my poor dragged muscles, while pictures of my father oiling the wheels of his mowing machine floated before my eyes.

All that remained to be done in the garden was to dress it with bark mulch and smarten up the paths with extra gravel. I had sourced well-rotted bark mulch that was soft

and pliable, and a truckload of it was dumped out at the garden gate. It was time to call in my Man for All Seasons. He arrived, bouncing with energy and enthusiasm as usual, to be welcomed with delight by Kate and Lolly. He drew barrow-loads up into the garden and upended them in regular heaps at strategic points, and I spread it out evenly, covering all irregularities with gorgeous black mulch. It was like wrapping a dark, soft, fur coat around the plants, flowers and trees, and as it slowly covered the garden it became a rich, dark carpet beneath the glowing greenery. It was an amazing transformation and, even better, it had the ancient smell of old wood. I walked around, sniffing with enjoyment, much to the amusement of Seasons, who decided that I was going soft in the head.

Next up was the gravel. This was a different experience entirely. Gravel is hard, sharp and unforgiving. I dragged it along with a rusty rake to the grating sound of iron against stone and the paths gradually lost their sags and hollows. They were getting a facelift, and when I was finished there was not a wrinkle in sight.

The garden was ready, but I was beginning to wilt. That night I took a long, warm soak in the bath and a miracle took place. I am a firm believer in bath magic: a shower is for cleansing, but a bath is a whole different experience. As the warm water gushed into the bath, I poured in my most expensive oils and bubbles, and I was very generous. This was no time for economy. No time for bright overhead lighting either: that's for the operating theatre! I lined the edges of the bath with softly glowing, scented candles. I pinned up an imaginary Do Not Disturb sign. I locked the door and submerged myself. Bliss.

Rejuvenation

Swirls of steam shroud the tired body
Of an old, old woman.
I crawl feebly over the bath edge
And submerge into the sudsy warmth.
My children are parasites,
My husband unloving,
My friends demanding;
I want to die.
My body dissolves,
My mind evaporates,
I become nothing,
Drifting into oblivion.
A few hot-water top-ups
And an hour later
I come back together.
My children are independent,
My husband adoring,
My friends supportive;

THE GIFT OF A GARDEN

It's good to be alive.
And I high-step
Out of the bath
Vibrant and beautiful
And the old lady
With all her problems
Disappears down
The plughole.

CHAPTER 17

THE OPEN GATE

It was the night before the grand opening. Kate and Lolly had been evicted to the dog kennels. They bounced unsuspectingly into the van without an anticipatory care in the world, and I was flooded with guilt. I simply could not accompany them to the kennels as I knew that as soon as Lolly saw the place she would adopt the I Shall Not Be Moved attitude, and I would feel even more guilty. She would act like an abandoned baby and my self-punishment would increase further. It was a lose, lose situation, so I chickened out and slunk back in through the garden gate as the van drove off with Lolly peering out through the back window. She is more finely tuned than Kate and had obviously begun to smell a rat. But there was no way they could stay around.

Despite the theme of the weekend, some visitors might be nervous around dogs and the mere sight of a dobermann can strike terror into the heart of the even most doggy-minded souls. So, having an open garden with two dobermann dogs on the loose was not an option. Despite all this reasoning and the strenuous efforts to convince myself that it was okay, I still felt bad. I needed a comforting, listening ear, so I rang a sister who loves gardening but not dogs. Bad decision! No comfort there: I shouldn't have dogs anyway if I was into gardening ...

I decided to make tea instead, and I cut myself a big wedge of fruitcake and took a tray out into the garden. Comfort eating. Just as I put the tray on the table the phone in the kitchen rang. Because Kate was absent it was safe to leave the tray unattended; if there, she would scoff the lot as she's a bad-mannered glutton. It was a small luxury. Lolly is a lady with the manners of a queen, whereas Kate behaves like Henry VIII, thinking everything in sight is hers. Here I was, I realised, still thinking of them though they were on their holidays. It must be the guilt. I decided to walk around the yard and garden and view the whole place as if I was one of tomorrow's visitors who had never seen the place.

Around the yard I had strategically placed pots on top of various holes in the old concrete around the edges to create the appearance of a hole-free zone. I examined it closely: it worked. The garden shed was next up for inspection. It has two windows through which enquiring eyes could normally view the working confusion of this gardener. Against the windows I had placed two painted canvases showing tranquil rustic scenes – obliterating the chaos inside. That worked too!

The garden itself was next up for inspection. Turning right at the gate, I began a slow, critical walk along the pathways. I read the information notices that I had earlier posted at strategic points telling visitors the story of the garden. I read the account of the old, iron garden chair that a blacksmith had made for me with horseshoes from Billy the Blacksmith's forge at the end of the village when Billy had died. Next, the history of the Old Hall that creates the northern boundary of the garden, and beside it the historic pathway leading down from the housing estate, The Spires, where the home of Winston Churchill's aunt, Clara Jerome Frewen, once stood. This pathway was used by the young Winston to access the river for fishing while he was on holiday with his aunt. Across the garden stood the stately *Jacquemontii* silver birch, which was a twenty-fifth silver wedding present in 1986; it had started off as a slender slip and is now a towering remembrance. This garden had inspired many poems and I had printed them out and pinned them at strategic points. Food for thought and time to contemplate. All these little fragments would tell the visitors the story of the garden. There is more to gardening than flowers, trees and shrubs. Every garden has its own story. I felt it was necessary to tell the visitors the story of this garden.

Deciding to open your garden to the public turns you into a weather forecast addict. You watch it on TV, listen to it on the radio, check it on your laptop, dial it on special telephone numbers sending your telephone bill sky high. My father used to simply stand on the doorstep, look up and read the night sky: he was his own free weather forecast service. He needed dry weather to save his hay and I needed it for my open garden. Only die-hard gardeners will traipse around a dripping garden, so if you want to attract the number of people that makes an open garden a worthwhile financial venture, fine weather is essential. This was a weekend opening, so my hope was for a good Saturday *and* Sunday. Was that too much to ask?

Saturday dawned soft and misty, which transformed the garden into a mystic, green, dripping wonderland. Beautiful, but not conducive to garden visiting I concluded. But I underestimated the real troopers who people the gardening world: in the gate they trudged, shrouded in an amazing array of all-encompassing rain wear – real gardeners pay no attention to the irrelevant detail of looking good, so they arrived donned in whatever it took to view the garden in comfort. I chatted with them and found out more about my own garden than I thought possible. It was like walking around the garden reading a hefty tome from the Royal Horticultural

Society. Gardeners are by nature generous, so their gardening knowledge is for every garden. We talked about the difficulties of dogs and how to overcome them; and I told people about my decision to abandon lawns completely because of Kate and Lolly. It was an enriching experience to chat with these wonderful gardeners and be enlightened by their wise recommendations. I hoped that they too got some ideas and inspiration from my humble efforts. The day slowly cleared and as the sun came out it melted the misty shroud over the garden, so that it glowed into sunlight. The day sped by, and I enjoyed every minute of it.

The following day the sun was high in the sky when we opened the gate – and people poured in. These were different to yesterday's brigade. Yesterday's people were real gardeners, these people were out for the day. The real gardeners had begun at the gate and worked their way methodically around the garden; the 'out for the day' people gave a general look around and then went and chatted to all and sundry. But everyone had come to enjoy themselves and on both days the garden and yard were full of laughter and conversation. Old friends met and many sat in the sun for long periods, catching up with local news. Young couples came and planned their own garden as they wandered around. Some enthusiastic gardening women arrived, dragging along reluctant husbands who were relieved to meet neighbouring men happy to discuss upcoming football and hurling matches. They parked themselves under the shade of a tree and talked about sports, the weather and farming. Later, one of them caught up with me. 'Do you know something,' he told me in surprised tone of voice, ''twas most enjoyable. Herself dragged me along and I didn't want to come at all.' 'Why not?' I asked. 'Don't you help out in the garden?' 'Ah, I thought the place would be full of women with posh accents and floppy hats,' he told me. 'Sure, they were all half-normal like myself!'

Mothers and daughters who enjoyed a shared interest in gardening came, and some women were accompanied by a daughter-in-law wise enough to benefit from the older woman's knowledge. People had travelled long distances, and because it was in aid of Tidy Towns some groups had come from towns in other counties, and, of course, dog owners had come to see what could be done with two dogs at large in a garden. When we finally closed the gate I had lost my voice and my legs were creaking at the joints, but I felt that life was wonderful and that if gardeners and dog owners were running the world it would be a very peaceful place indeed. But it was time to bring Kate and Lolly home.

CHAPTER 18

THE *MEITHEAL*

'The best time to plant a tree is twenty years ago;
the next best time is now.'

Boundaries have always caused problems. Where my piece of land finishes and yours begins has forever been a thorny dilemma in Ireland. The same problem has led to global warfare. However, in Innishannon if you should decide to extend your garden boundary out around the village you are more than welcome to do so. You may well ask, why would you want do that? Well, there is really no answer, only to say that real gardeners are a strange breed in that

gardening is not about land ownership but rather about till-
ing the soil and making the earth smile with flowers. Once
you take that first step outside your own front door and put
out window boxes, you have stepped through the invisible
glass wall between you and the rest of the world. In a village,
the next step is planting up street tubs, troughs and waste
areas and from there on, the horizon is the limit!

On the approach road into our village, which is on the
main road from Cork city to West Cork, there was for many
years a long track of wasteland, sporting weeds, abandoned
tar left over after road repairs, and rubbish. Because rubbish
invites more rubbish, it was fast turning into a dump, and an
embarrassment. After all, who wants a dump outside their
front door? And this was effectively the front door of our
village. So the answer was planting. As this was a large tract
of land between the main road and a side road, it did not
lend itself to fancy plants and flowers, so the obvious solution was trees; it definitely was a site for the heavyweights of
the garden world. It was also a golden opportunity, a time to
remember the wisdom of the Kenyan environmental activist
Wangari Maathai. She said: 'Until you dig a hole, you plant
a tree, you water it and make it survive, you haven't done a
thing. You are just talking.' It was time to quit talking.

So how were we in the Tidy Towns committee to fund this
enterprise? Good trees cost money – and we were thinking
big, with well developed, ball-rooted trees in mind. It made

for a far more expensive tree, but we were paying for years of growth. We were in one sense buying time. This is not always possible and in normal circumstances not necessary, but we felt that in this particular project it would be a worthwhile investment.

Most people like the idea of planting a tree, so we asked the locals if they would like to sponsor a tree in our new grove. The response was heart-warming and contributions flowed in. If you think about it, planting a tree is probably the cheapest and best investment you will make in life. The tree will grow stronger from the first day it hits the soil and will, if some fool does not get a chainsaw to it, outlive you for centuries, enhancing and enriching the earth long after you have ceased to matter. We plant flowers and shrubs for ourselves, but we plant trees for the next generation.

Then, a visit to our local tree farm was a delightful experience where Matthew, the tree man, extolled the virtues and the limitations of the different species. When I inquired about the choice of a specific tree, it was quickly dismissed as a 'Mickey Mouse' type, so from then on we decided we would be guided by his expertise. It was amazing to watch an enormous circular saw penetrate deep into the ground beneath each tree and cut out a huge ball around the roots so that the tree would be moved with minimum disturbance.

We had enough money to hire machinery to clear the site and draw in good topsoil. You only get one chance to give a tree a good home and if you miss that opportunity you will watch the poor tree struggle for years. We piled in old horse dung that would provide years of future nourishment. We were determined to give our trees the best possible start in life. The evening before the big planting was mild and the tree bed was dressed and ready. Golden brown earth, like a huge velvet duvet, stretched out over soft blankets of the rich, warm horse dung that lay waiting to receive the trees. 'It's like a bridal bed,' I enthused to a neighbouring farmer who had joined me to view it in the gathering dusk. 'Ah Alice,' he protested, 'you're losing the run of yourself!'

But excitement coursed through my veins as I viewed our wonderful achievement and the prospect of things to come. The eyesore at the entrance to our lovely village had been removed and now the thought of a future grove was a thrilling prospect. There can be nothing more satisfying for the human soul than planting a tree, and to be planting over twenty trees in one go was almost too much to take in. On such occasions I always think of Uncle Jacky and the blessings he left behind in his garden. And now here were these trees waiting to be planted. They would enrich and calm the heart of all who, in future years, would pass by – and as thirteen thousand vehicles pass by here daily, that would be a lot of people!

The following day I awoke at dawn to the sound of rain pounding off the roof. But this did not take the edge off

my excitement. One of the great things about an exciting project is that you wake up full of anticipation. It happens to me if I am painting a picture, planning a planting or writing about something I love, as I am now. It probably all comes down to creativity in flow – we dance with creativity and with creation itself.

Out the road in the grove, hooded people in long, waterproof gear were digging holes at specified locations. This was the old Irish *meitheal* system at work. The *meitheal* way of doing things dates far back into the Irish farming culture: if there was a job to be done that needed a large workforce, many neighbours came together to help, and then you did likewise for them. It was a great system, with many hands making light of the work, and in the process bringing companionship and bonding to the community. Most of our diggers were farmers who are used to working in all kinds of weather, so they took it in their stride. The trees were lined up in a trailer beside the road and then lifted into the holes when they were judged deep enough to contain the root balls in comfort. Men and women dug the holes and then gently put the trees to bed – in gardening there is no gender discrimination. Wellington boots sank into the soft earth and much good-humoured banter greeted anyone unfortunate enough to get stuck and who had to be hand-lifted out. Gradually the holes were filled. The day cleared up and tea arrived in wheelbarrows.

When a *meitheal* is out working, there is nothing they enjoy more than a break for sustenance. Mugs were filled out of large teapots and hungry workers sank their teeth into generous sandwiches and homemade cakes. More than half the trees were in by now and we soon returned to work with renewed vigour. By late afternoon all the trees were standing. And what a glorious sight it was! Then, because tree planting is a sacred event, we were joined by our two clergymen, Church of Ireland and Catholic, to bless the trees. There is no religious discrimination in nature either. Together we all bowed our heads in thanksgiving. We had much to be grateful for.

Having got the taste of communal tree planting and the transformation that it brought about, other waste areas around the village came under scrutiny. Across the road from our grove was a long, sloping bank of mainly scrub and furze bushes. These bushes are lovely in the spring, but are not very hospitable to trees as they have no manners and shoulder the trees out of their way, eventually stifling them. However, once trees would get going and become firmly established, they could hold their own. We eyed this bank as a potential wooded area too, but it was three times the length and twice the width of the grove, so would need to be tackled in stages. But everything in gardening and planting takes time, and nature is mostly a slow mover. We were not daunted by the challenge and soon the digger returned to clear the scrub.

Here we had to think big as the first planting would be a hundred trees. On this occasion, ball-rooted trees were not even considered as financial resources were limited. We settled for much younger trees, which was wiser in any case as the soil here was far poorer. This long bank had been created by the local council in the widening of the road long, long before my time. Uncle Jacky had talked about this soil as consisting of clay and stones and a local farmer had told me: 'That bloody place wouldn't even grow grass.' So we had our work cut out for us.

On a cold, bleak Easter Saturday morning, we began the planting. We got off to a very shaky start, and even considered cancelling due to the wintry conditions – but shortly after the appointed time my phone rang and a harassed voice demanded, 'Where the hell are ye all?' 'Well, we were thinking of cancelling,' I told him hesitantly. 'What? Why the hell?' he demanded. 'Sure, the rain is good for the trees.'

You could not argue with that, so I assured him that he would soon have help. I rounded up the usual suspects and a reluctant crew slowly gathered on the hill. Once we got going, progress was made and as the trees did not have a large rooting system the holes required were not very big. Still, the ground was hard and stony, and not easy to penetrate, and patches of it were soft and soggy. One of our workers sank up to his knees in one of these patches and we had to lift him out, leaving his wellingtons behind; these had to be dug out then. He was not amused. 'This is the nearest thing to slave labour I've ever endured,' he informed us.

But the arrival of the tea cheered everyone up and after that progress was rapid. More helpers joined us on the hill as the word had gone out that crazy people were out the road planting in the rain. There is nothing like the village bush telegraph. Come evening the hundred trees were standing, but such is the size of that hilly bank that we knew there would be another day the following year. And indeed last year, on a lovely, bright spring day we planted another hundred trees, and because the weather was good and the sun was shining there was laughter and smiles all around. It's amazing the difference a sunny day can make. Gradually our wooded entrance to the village was coming into being.

Then along the approach roads closer to the village we planted beech hedging. Beech is a lovely russet brown winter hedge, which in spring transforms itself into a vivid sap green. In damp, shady areas inhospitable to many types of plant, we set hydrangeas that thrive in shade and in damp conditions. In the plant world there is one for every type of location. Keeping them happy is the name of the game. It's all about location, location, location.

Then the gods smiled on us and word came through on the grapevine that the Secret of West Cork garden centre were looking for a home for twenty mature oaks as they were redesigning their space; they wanted to know if we could use them. We could not believe our luck! So, Stephen, a local lad with a digger prepared the holes and early one morning Peter and Doug collected the oaks in a trailer and into the holes they went the same day. They were fine trees of about ten years' growth, and really made a statement at the entrance to the village.

Our *meitheal* had dug a hole – over a hundred times – planted a tree in each one, watered it and made it survive, so we had done something. We were not just talking!

Chapter 19

WILD-FLOWER GARDEN

'The evil that men do lives after them;
The good oft interred with their bones.'

I would not usually disagree with what must be one of the keenest brains in literary history, but on this occasion I beg to differ with William Shakespeare. I believe that the joys people leave behind when they depart this world very often light up the paths for us who come after them. A few days ago, on a stroll along the village to the old graveyard down by the river, I stopped to admire a wonderful window box planted by a woman who had actually passed away earlier in the year. Since then, her box had stood untouched but for the odd jug of water occasionally poured into it by a neighbour. Now it was full of vibrant flowers, a loving reminder of a green-fingered lady. As I passed, I prayed that her heaven was full of flowers.

That is why I find it wonderful to see old graveyards blooming with flowers. These forgotten places are havens of peace and sanctuaries for wildlife. In our village we have such a retreat in a hidden corner down by the river at the end of the village. For many years there had been no access to this forgotten graveyard as a tree had grown up through the rusty entrance gate and clung it to the ground. Nobody had ventured in there for years, except those fit enough to scale the high stone wall. Nature had reclaimed it for her own and the headstones were suffocated in greenery. Out of this green oasis rose an old tower and at its shoulder an ancient, upright yew.

A group of us decided to do a reclamation job on this forgotten graveyard and after a summer of nightly forays into this impenetrable jungle, access was finally achieved and the old graveyard became an extension of the village. Here, tilted headstones dating back centuries added interest to leisurely strolls; and here, for historical reasons, many denominations are buried side by side: French Huguenots and Irish Catholics and Protestants all lie peacefully together. There is no religious discrimination amongst the dead.

The ruin of the old church dates back to 1225 and the old tower was added in 1750. Though not a total ruin, the tower too was showing the wear and tear of the centuries. In the course of our work on the grounds we cleared out a little side chapel that had been built for the Huguenots. There were decades of debris in there and when we finally reached base after weeks of digging and clearing, we were amazed to find tombstones lining the floor. On reading the inscriptions, we discovered they were those of the minister who had served here in 1856 and his family. It was at that date that a new Protestant church was built in the village and the minister had obviously acquired the old church as a family vault. I would never claim to be an archaeologist, but on that evening I think I discovered how they must feel when they have a successful dig. On hands and knees we cleaned out the grooves of the writing on the old stones and followed the ancient script with our fingers. We discovered that many children lay buried in this little chapel. It was poignant. We were walking on sacred ground.

When all the clearing was done, we decided to turn the whole graveyard into a wild-flower meadow. I had always dreamt of having of a wild-flower garden, and here, beneath the wood and beside the river, we had the perfect location. And everyone could share it. I had this romantic idea, though, that you simply had to scatter the seeds with free abandon and – hey presto! – drifts of wild flowers soon emerged,

waving in the breeze. I read wild-flower gardening books full of fabulous pictures of colourful meadows overflowing with flowers. Poor soil, apparently, was a prerequisite, and as our graveyard was rocky and rough, we seemed to have the ideal conditions.

We scattered the wild-flower seeds and held our breaths. Nothing – for weeks. Then the weeks turned into months. Then very slowly little bits of what looked like weeds began to appear. They did not look very promising. Some were tall and others were tiny, and overall the place looked like a neglected patch – almost as neglected as it had been before we began our work. I began to despair and for a little while skipped my daily visits as they were depressing me. Then one sunny morning I went down to the graveyard – and a miracle had happened. The entire place had burst into a riot of glowing colour. It was breathtaking. The whole village came to see it. That first summer, our old graveyard was a joy to behold. On one lovely August day I saw three artists there, strategically seated at their easels, busily committing images of our wild flowers to canvas.

I knew nothing about wild-flower gardening, but over the next few years I learnt a lot. Anyone who tells you that it is a trouble-free way of gardening never did it. The first year is a joy, but then wild grass and weeds decide to compete with the flowers and shoulder them out of the way. Eventually these persistent weeds, if not restrained, get the better of the gentle flowers. The maxim 'the price of freedom is eternal vigilance' most definitely applies here. In the end, because we could not provide the eternal vigilance needed, we had to strike a balance, and when the weeds and grass seemed to be winning the battle over the flowers, we came to the rescue. So we settled for a less than perfect wild-flower graveyard – which was still very beautiful.

Then disaster struck and part of the old tower collapsed, and so the County Council locked the gate for safety reasons – and nature reclaimed our wild-flower garden. But hope springs eternal in the gardening breast, so one day I know that, with the restoration of the tower, wild flowers will once again bloom in our old graveyard garden, and I will be the first artist in with paints and palette to commit them to canvas.

CHAPTER 20

ROOTS

Some trees grow tall quickly and fail to put down deep roots. When the storms come, they topple over. Nature teaches us the value of roots and the longer I garden the more I learn to appreciate them. The old apple tree that Uncle Jacky planted over a hundred years ago remains unbending in the storms and I sense that its roots are spread out deep beneath the whole garden. As the lifespan of a tree can be hundreds of years – the trees in the Garden of Olives are there since the time of Christ – Jacky's apple tree may not even be a senior citizen yet. But one of the reasons that I love my garden is its sense of timelessness and deep connection with the past. It is also the reason that I love our village, Innishannon, too. Its roots stretch back to the sixth century.

There was a village here before bridges were built, when a little ford across the river was the only entrance to West Cork. The village grew up around that ford at a time when river crossings were of great importance to the survival of people and animals. People walked across our river, which is tidal, when the water had withdrawn downstream to Kinsale harbour. The laneway that led to this ford is know as Bóthairín an Átha: little road to the ford. Here travellers on foot and on horseback forded the river and one wonders at what point in time they were joined by carriages. An other world prevailed here then, completely different to the whirring traffic that today spins past this little secluded laneway that is still hidden at the end of our village. Now we are into high-speed traffic, but centuries ago our ancestors travelled here on foot and on horseback.

We decided that our village would be enriched by a defining statement at its main entrance, alerting approaching traffic that they were travelling in ancient footsteps. But how best to commemorate this ancient past? We needed a statement that spoke volumes, and we decided on a horse. A horse would stamp her hooves outside our village and wake everyone up and remind them they were passing through a historic place. Before Innishannon bridge was built in 1695 and Bandon bridge in 1594, the horse was the one who had crossed the river at low tide. It was she who walked or trotted down the narrow laneway, across the river and along a dirt track that is now gone, and made her way into Bandon town and onwards to West Cork.

As Innishannon was the only gateway into West Cork for a very long time, it was a place of immense commercial importance, and got a royal charter as far back as 1412, two hundred years before Cork city got its charter. In fact, our home place was first mentioned in the Book of Leinster in the sixth century, and later we were wrecked by the Vikings in the ninth century. So we had old, old stories to tell. Stories can be conveyed in print, or orally, or visually. In this case we opted for the visual. But the image chosen needed to have clarity, depth and significance, paying tribute to many centuries. And who better to tell our story than the horse?

In my opinion, each city, town and village needs a stamp of identity at its entrance. Just as a gate or doorway makes a statement about a house, so too does the approach road into a village. Out there, a visual impact is required, to announce to the visitor the story of the place they are about to enter. We already had a story at our back door where a sculpture, 'Billy the Blacksmith', announces that this ancient craft was practised here for generations. I like to think of our village as a rambling garden and now we were about to put up a garden gate, be it an open one. Up to now our garden gate, though well maintained and wooded, could be the entrance to any village. We needed something unique, our own stamp. We wanted something strong, dramatic and visually arresting,

which could, at the same time, carry a depth of meaning carved deep by centuries of time. But how do you tell such a story? In these circumstances you turn to creativity, genius and vision.

We are blessed that we have such a genius living amongst us, one who could tell our story in a form that would stand the test of time. Don Cronin, who created the sculpture 'Billy the Blacksmith' to such perfection that he is beyond criticism, would now come on board to create another masterpiece: a horse that would make a statement. Not an elegant Coolmore Stud-type of horse, but one honed by centuries of time, one who would breathe antiquity from another era. This was the challenge – and the dream to which Don was to give substance. Actually, we discovered that it had always been his dream to sculpt a horse; now it was also our village dream.

But sculptures cost money and in recent times the price of all the components had rocketed, and so we checked our sources of income. Our starting point was the profits from our local Christmas publication, *Candlelight*, which had already helped to fund 'Billy the Blacksmith'. These funds by themselves were insufficient, but they were a stepping stone into assistance from West Cork Development Partnership (WCDP), who would grant-aid us if we could match their commitment – and we could!

Eventually we got to the starting gate and Don began

the long road of sculpting our horse and rider. Unless you observe it first-hand, it is difficult to imagine the amount of sheer hard work and absolute drudgery that goes into the sculpting of a major piece of work. The original outline, which necessitates genius and vision, shows an image of the finished product, but that is only the beginning and only the first step on a long road of physically demanding work – lifting, dipping and casting. At one stage our horse existed in fifty-eight pieces and one wondered how all this was going to come together. This work took place during the ferocious winter of 2010-11 and, just as you cannot garden in minus ten degrees, neither can you sculpt. But when the thaw came, work resumed. Watching it all come about was like witnessing a miracle happen. On the day that we first saw 'Horse and Rider' all in one piece in the Sculpture Factory in Cork city we were gobsmacked with delight, and a man who happened to pass by, looked up at her in awe and gasped: 'What a statement!' And that is exactly what she would be.

Back in the village, preparations for the horse's arrival were afoot. To accompany our sculpture, we planned a historic guide map at the corner of the village, with matching plaques on historic houses around the village and an accompanying brochure. My neighbours Jerry and Gavin and I put hours of research and planning into these, and Sign Spec, also in the parish, did a wonderful production job. The end result is a beautiful series of informative plaques and brochures for an

interesting walk around the village, beginning at the horse. All this cost money, of course, and I did my bit by opening my garden for a weekend. To what better use can you put a garden than to fund a dream?

Prior to the big day, 9 July 2011, a huge effort was made by the entire village to look good. Every house put out window boxes and every scruffy corner of the village was improved – it was a bit like an 'open garden' of the whole village. The site for 'Horse and Rider' was made ready and all the grass on the approach roads manicured. As the big day approached, the village began to look better and better.

Then one day at early-morning Mass, a neighbour whispered across to me: 'The horse is out the road.' Her voice was full of delight and amazement. I was out the door before the priest left the altar, and I tore up the road. There, hidden in the trees by the grove, perched high on a trailer, was our magnificent horse, carrying her cloaked rider, calmly waiting for her horsemen to bear her into her permanent stable. I danced around her in delight. She looked wonderful. Soon the forces assembled, and with much manoeuvring and edging backwards and forwards, she was eased into place on her bronze plinth, where she was firmly secured. She was shrouded in black plastic. But on the morning of her big day, she would be dressed for the occasion. Next, a long marquee appeared for the festivities. A stage was erected for the official unveiling. Weather forecasts were checked hourly – perhaps someone even put out the Child of Prague statue to guarantee good weather as our parents might have done?

The morning of Saturday, 9 July dawned bright and beautiful. It was time to dress the bride. Her dramatic cloak had been designed and created by Elfie, who lives nearby and normally creates bridal wear – this surely was her largest bridal gown ever! Our superstar was stripped of her black wrapping and donned her gorgeous, flowing ruby gown. She glowed with magnificence. The village also glowed and held its breath. We were looking good! Transformed village windows had stepped back in time: out had come old photographs and family memorabilia, and people walked from window to window taking a trip down memory lane. Vintage cars were parked along the kerb and caressed lovingly by enthusiasts while eye-popping children climbed on board. An old gramophone coughed out slow waltzes at the bottom of the village. Quietly, people from another era began to appear along the street – bonneted ladies in flowing skirts, cloaked women carrying baskets, little girls in long, floral dresses and young garsoons in short pants and caps, elegant gentlemen with gaiters and bowler hats walked sedately along. We had gone back to the time of the horse.

Then the pipe band marched in their colourful regalia down the hill from St Mary's church and at the corner gave a pulsating performance, then led the whole village, in their gowns, hats and parasols, towards the waiting, cloaked horse. We halted at Bóthairín an Átha where the band played a tribute to the source of all our celebrations.

When all had gathered on the green, proceedings commenced, and when the ruby cloak slid to the ground, an involuntary gasp of appreciation rose from the crowd as our 'Horse and Rider' made their first public appearance. They breathed antiquity. Angled towards Bóthairín an Átha, the horse and cloaked, barefoot rider looked totally at one with their wooded background. People wanted to rub her, feel her, measure themselves against her and look up at her in awe. Cameras flashed and entire families gathered around her to be photographed beside her. She was a star, and a magnificent one.

We remembered all the great people who over the centuries had travelled down Bóthairín an Átha. This sculpture was a tribute to their endurance and strength. We were here because they had built up our village by the river. Later, it was pronounced by all to have been a great day. But by far the greatest part of the day was the fact that now at the entrance to Innishannon we have a fitting statement telling all that this is a village with an old, old history. A garden gate into a place in which it is good to live.

CHAPTER 21

PLANTING MIRACLES

Waking up with the sun warm on your face is a wonderful welcome into a new day – and when that morning happens to be the last Monday in October, it is also a loving farewell kiss from departing autumn. It is the last bank holiday weekend of 2012, and I have planned a bulb-planting day. The timing is perfect. We are on the skirt tails of autumn and awaiting a far-distant spring, which is as yet simply a hopeful seed that will later flower in our minds. But this is to be a day full of the future. Bulbs are little power-houses of promise and planting them is an act of trust in the hidden wonder of nature.

For three days large bags of daffodil and tulip bulbs have rested on the table in my back porch. Every time I eye them as I pass in and out to the garden, they glow with promise. Through their yellow net bags, their soft cream and amber hues smile beguilingly at me. They plead gently with me: put us into the soft brown earth so that we can begin our journey into next spring. As I keep putting the day on the long finger, they fill me with guilt. But now I can clear my conscience because this is the day, a perfect day for planting. My bulbs are about to begin their journey.

A deluge of a summer has blossomed into a golden October, transforming the trees on the wooded hills around our village into a cascading profusion of burnt oranges, fiery reds and golden ambers. Nature had obviously decided to erode the memory of the wet summer with a stunning autumn finale. And today I am going to join that final chorus line by donning my gardening gloves and my apron of many pockets and getting out there to prepare for the spring. The inevitable hunt for the right garden trowel will begin as soon as breakfast is over.

Before heading downstairs to the kitchen, I climb the high stairs to the attic to view Dromkeen Wood on the hillside across the river from our house. This wood was originally planted in 1750 by an ambitious landlord who actually laid out contrasting trees so that his name would be emblazoned across the hill above our village! But time has eroded his efforts to stamp his identity on the countryside, and the trees on this October morning blend together in a multi-coloured

indistinguishable huddle above the soft clouds of mist swirling along the river valley. I have spent a lot of time over
the years up here in this attic, writing, and I am constantly
drawn to the view from this roof-top window. I never cease
to marvel at the changing faces that the seasons bring to
this wood. You wait for it to shine green in spring and then
gradually swell into the profusion of summer, then slowly
glow into autumn and finally turn pale for winter. The wood
tells the story of the year, but every year the story differs
somewhat as the weather dictates the colours and textures
that each tree will don for the changing seasons.

But this autumn has surpassed all others for its wealth of
colour. Now, as I soak in the wonder of the wood, two swans
rise from the river and glide downstream. Even from this
distance I can hear the strong beat of their wings. I feel that
swans that are so elegant on water and waddle awkwardly on
land, come into their own in the air when their real strength
comes into force. I love watching them fly. Like giant aircraft,
their powerful wings send out magnetic vibrations as their
long necks thrust forward, slicing the air. Swans must surely
have been the inspiration for flight design. But, as a friend
of mine says when I dilly dally instead of getting down to
work, 'This will never keep white stockings on the Missus,'
so I head downstairs and after breakfast I crack into action.

The window boxes out at the front of the house will be
my first port of call. But before going out there I need to

organise myself, so I get three large brown paper bags and mark one 'red tulips', the second 'yellow tulips' and the third 'daffodils'. Having opened my net bags, I fill the three paper bags with the colour-coded bulbs and place the entire collection in a basket that a friend of mine made for me many years ago. I absolutely love baskets and the fact that somebody made this one specially for me gives me an extra sense of well-being every time I use it. Now for the trowel. Surprise, surprise, I find it quickly – the one I need is on the sill of the back window above my ancient earthenware sink. Long and narrow, this trowel is the perfect bulb planter. I take my cargo out the front door and line it up beside the window to the right of the door.

Then back out again into the backyard for the real treasure that is going to work wonders for these bulbs. Here in the garden shed are two bags of richly rotted, mature horse dung. I stumbled across this vintage enricher the previous week when out tracing the history of a local castle. At the end of a narrow, rutted lane was a riding stables, and there in all its glory was a mountain of the most beautiful horse dung that I had ever laid eyes on. It was glorious! It would make Monty Don and Helen Dillon froth at the mouth with envy. These horses had been bedded in sawdust; now the sawdust and the dung were well rotted together with a moist, golden wine seeping through the layers. I felt my blood pressure rise with excitement. The horses, whose heads looked out over

half-doors all around the yard, neighed with the excitement of seeing me, and I nearly joined in with the thrill of seeing their contribution to my gardening world. Mary, who owns the stables, assured me that it was there for the taking. Sometimes the best things in life *are* free. So now, in my garden shed, I carefully shovel out my golden, moist horse dung into a bucket and bring it out to join the basket. Ready for action! When I get my act together I can be very organised.

Last year's primulas are in residence in the window boxes, so they have to be tidied up and made receptive to their new neighbours. I dig out the tired old soil around them and give it a gee-up with my wonderful new tonic. The worms burrow down into the new territory. Each time I see this activity I remind myself how much I love worms. They are the wires that carry the current through the soil, giving life to plants. When all is rejuvenated I take out my bulbs and place them generously around the box. There is no place for any *ocras*, or want, in bulb planting, as generosity is the name of a good display. A strong, eye-catching mix of red and yellow tulips and miniature daffodils that won't fall over in the spring, that's what I'm after. As I plant I visualise them pushing up their inquiring little noses during the cold, bleak days of January and February. Spring bulbs are the beacons that light our way out of bleak winter.

With one box done, I could think – if I did not know better – that I'd have the front boxes finished by lunchtime, but I remember from previous experience that this will not be the case. Planting on the side of the street attracts gardeners, and indeed non-gardeners, like bees to a honey pot. It can be a very sociable pursuit, depending on your frame of mind, and also on the people who happen to come by. Most people are generally interested and interesting, but you also get the 'geniuses' who think that they are simply hilarious by suggesting that 'When you are finished there, come up and do mine.' On third hearing, I could quite happily shovel some of my valuable horse dung down their throats!

With the sun warm on my back and the non-stop traffic floating past behind me, I am as happy as a pig in muck. Planting bulbs is surely one of the most energy-enhancing pursuits in gardening. But gradually my back begins to complain. I change from the upright to the 'leaning tower of Pisa' position, but soon that begins to takes its toll too. I down tools and massage my aching lower back. Time for a break. It is at times like this that you would love somebody to put their head around the door and announce invitingly: Lunch is ready. But no such luck. Rather than drag everything in, I leave all in situ. Over the years I have found that no light-fingered, mean-spirited passers-by have ever helped themselves to my abandoned gardening bits and pieces. It restores my trust in our fellow human beings.

By evening, all the ground-floor window boxes have been completed. To the casual passer-by, they look no different than they did that morning, but I know they hold a secret, hidden treasure. In a few months' time, this treasure will bloom into a rainbow of vibrant colours proclaiming that spring is here. I give them all a good watering. Job done! Nature will do the rest. It is no wonder that gardeners believe in God.

OTHER BOOKS BY
Alice Taylor

AND TIME STOOD STILL

Alice Taylor shares her heart and soul, her loves and losses in this intimate book
Alice has known, loved, and lost many people throughout her life. Here
she talks about her special people, her memory of what meant so much
to her about them. She remembers her husband, father and mother, a
beloved sister, her little brother Connie, and many others. She tells how
she coped with the emptiness she felt when they died, of the seeming
impossibility of moving on with life after such deeply felt loss, when time
stood still.

TO SCHOOL THROUGH THE FIELDS

Twenty-five years after its first publication, this new illustrated edition
celebrates Alice Taylor's first book, a much-loved bestseller
and a true classic.

Life in rural 1940s and 50s Ireland: on the farm working with horses, rearing and growing the family's food; an old-world life of self-sufficiency, friendship and, above all, neighbourliness. The walk to school was challenging but often delightful, with many stops along to way for sustenance or entertainment, at a time when children could roam free.

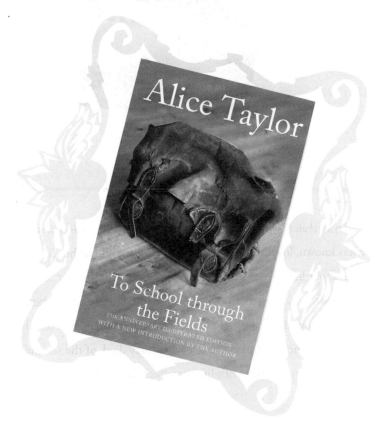

ALICE TAYLOR

Quench The Lamp

BY THE AUTHOR OF "TO SCHOOL THROUGH THE FIELDS"

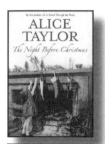

By the author of To School Through the Fields

ALICE TAYLOR

The Night Before Christmas

Alice Taylor

a Country Miscellany

ALICE TAYLOR

Country Days

BY THE AUTHOR OF "TO SCHOOL THROUGH THE FIELDS"

From the bestselling author of To School Through the Fields

ALICE TAYLOR

THE VILLAGE

"There is charm and humour in The Village as well as a quality perhaps best described as loving kindness."
Limin Independent

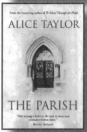

From the bestselling author of To School Through the Fields

ALICE TAYLOR

THE PARISH

"Her writing is balm to the soul in these mad commercialised times."
Ireland

ALICE TAYLOR

THE JOURNEY

NEW AND SELECTED POEMS

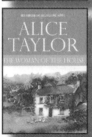

ALICE TAYLOR

THE WOMAN OF THE HOUSE

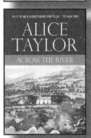

ALICE TAYLOR

ACROSS THE RIVER

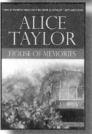

ALICE TAYLOR

HOUSE OF MEMORIES

AN EVENING WITH ALICE TAYLOR

Alice Taylor's selection, in her own voice, from her memories and thoughts of childhood and country life.

90 MINUTES

BRANDON